Mw

Generational Wealth

Beginner's Business & Investing Guide
Third Edition

LaFoy Orlando Thomas III, Esq.

This book does not take the place of hired financial or legal advice and does not create an attorney-client relationship. All information in this book is subject to change without notice and should be viewed as a general, not definitive, guide.

Contents

Chapter I

Introduction

The need for education on business and investing has never been more important than it is today. Whether it is in real estate, stocks, or investing your life savings into a small business, positioning our money in an environment where it can grow is a necessity if wealth is to be attained. It is no secret that people who have aspirations to become wealthy consistently spend their money on assets that are likely to appreciate in value and produce a positive cash flow.

On the other hand, many of those without a basic education in business or finance will often spend their hard-earned money on futile possessions that have little to no chance of ever producing income or having an appreciated resale value.

I can't stress how important it is to do something positive with your hard-earned money instead of spending it on futile possessions, such as luxury cars or expensive clothing. It's not that you can't have these nice things, I'm only suggesting that you don't spend your hard-earned money to get them. Instead, spend your hard-earned money on an asset, such as a dividend paying stock, which produces a positive cash flow that you can then spend however you please.

Chapter 2

The Importance of Economics

How well a particular investment performs is generally influenced by the state of the economy. Before learning about a specific investment, it is essential to learn about the economy and the impact that it has on the world of investing. Also, it is very important to know what part of the economic cycle you are in and know how to adjust and react to each climate accordingly.

The economy is measured by several economic indicators that take the temperature of the economy, and some indicators even give a forecast of what is expected of the economy in the future.

Of all the economic indicators, some are more important than others. The most important economic indicator is considered by many as the parent indicator, and that is the gross domestic product (GDP). The GDP is the total dollar value of all goods and services produced by labor and property in the United States. It measures total consumer spending, private domestic investments, government spending, and net exports.

A GDP that is increasing signifies an economic growth cycle that may cause inflation, and a GDP on the decline signifies an economy that is slowing down and may have the potential to cause deflation. Inflation is the rise of prices for goods and services; deflation is the decrease in prices for goods and services.

The GDP report measures quarterly activity and has a heavy influence on how people invest and spend their money. The report is released three times each quarter, being revised each time to finally come up with a final report for the quarter during the last month of the next quarter. For example, the final revision of the GDP report for the first quarter (January-March) would be released in June. The first estimate of a quarter is called the advance estimate and it is released during the last week of the first month following the end of the quarter. The GDP figure is then revised during the following month and is considered a preliminary estimate. The second and final revision, which is released a month after the preliminary estimate, is called the final estimate.

Keeping track of the GDP growth (or decline) numbers should give you a good feel for the state of the economy and also let you know what phase of the business or economic cycle you are currently in. There are generally four phases in the business cycle, which are described below.

Business Cycle

1.) **Downturn:** Starting from the peak in the economy, the downturn starts when the GDP has its first quarter of negative growth and lasts for as long as the GDP report is signifying negative growth. Two consecutive quarters of negative GDP growth is officially considered a recession. During a downturn, investors generally get nervous and begin to dump quality investments for less than fair value. At this time, investment bargains are usually easy to find.

2.) **Trough:** The trough signifies the end of the downturn or recession. It represents the lowest level in the business cycle. During a trough, because it is the lowest phase in the cycle, reports start to improve and the economy is getting ready to bounce back. In my opinion, this is the best time to invest, especially in real estate and stocks. Due to a lack of consumer and investor confidence at this point in the cycle, investments are usually relatively inexpensive, and I advise investors to buy as much quality real estate and stocks as possible.

3.) **Expansion:** The recovery begins when GDP growth is positive again and continues until it reaches a new peak. A recovery technically becomes an expansion when the level of GDP surpasses the previous peak in GDP. Expansions are often accompanied by stock bull markets, which can make it very difficult to find good companies that are trading at fair valuations.

4.) **Peak:** The peak is the highest point in the business cycle. In my opinion, this is the worst time to start investing. At the peak of a business cycle, the Federal Reserve will usually raise interest rates to slow down the economy or to prevent rapid inflation in home prices and both the housing and stock markets usually lose steam when interest rates rise.

Important Economic Indicators

Although there are many economic indicators viewed and adhered to by Wall Street, there are only 10 of them besides the GDP report that I find important, and they are listed below. It is important to understand that most economic indicators are subject to monthly revisions; therefore, be aware that the GDP reading is not the only indicator that is subject to changes once more data is received by the source of the economic report.

In addition to reading any particular economic report, it is a good idea to also read any analysis of the report, which can usually be found on CNBC.com and Bloomberg.com. This should help you become more familiar with the reports and to have an understanding of how to utilize them in your trading or investing efforts.

1.) **Consumer Price Index (CPI):** The CPI measures the level of inflation or increase in prices for goods and services in the marketplace. When examining this report, it's good to look at the overall number and the Core Consumer Price Index, which excludes price increases for food and energy—which are considered pretty volatile. Inflation is generally high during times of an expansion and lower during a downturn. During an expansion, people and businesses are spending money at new levels, and the high demand for goods and services generally allows businesses to raise their prices. Generally, when inflation is growing too rapidly, the Federal Reserve (Federal Open Market Committee) will take action and raise interest rates, which will make money not as easy to borrow. The CPI report is released monthly, approximately two weeks after the month ends.

2.) **Employment Report:** The employment report, which is officially titled The Employment Situation, contains information such as the unemployment rate, payrolls, and hourly wages. This report is very important as it is one of the first indicators each month of which direction the economy is going. In times of an expansion or growing economy, payrolls are usually up, and the unemployment rate is usually down and vice versa for times of a downturn or a recession. As was the case during the Great Recession, when consumers are out of work, the economy suffers because of it. This report is also released monthly on the first Friday of every month.

3.) **Weekly Jobless Claims:** The weekly jobless claims report, which officially is titled the Unemployment Insurance Weekly Claims Report, is released every Thursday and is closely followed by investors. This indicator reports the number of initial claims for unemployment insurance and the number of continuing claims for unemployment insurance. The weekly average is considered to be pretty volatile from week to week, and many investors focus their attention on the four-week average for a more accurate picture of any underlying employment trends. The weekly jobless claims report is considered a leading economic indicator, which means claims tend to rise before a recession and tend to fall prior to a recovery.

4.) **Retail Sales:** The Retail Sales report, which officially is titled the Advance Monthly Sales for Retail and Food Services, measures sales of retail firms, such as car dealerships, clothing stores, gas stations, and grocery stores, that sell to consumers. The retail sales report is one of the most important reports as it gives us a good indication of consumer spending, which accounts for approximately 70% of the gross domestic product. Generally, when retail sales are strong, inflation shortly follows as it shows an increased demand for consumer goods. This report is usually released in the middle of every month.

5.) **Consumer Confidence:** The Consumer Confidence Index, which is officially titled The Conference Board Consumer Confidence Index, gives a reflection of how consumers feel about the current and future state of the economy or business cycle. A decrease in consumer confidence usually causes a decrease in consumer spending and, therefore, a decrease in the GDP. When consumers are not comfortable about the current or future state of the economy, they usually tighten their belts and decrease their level of spending due to worries that hard times may be coming ahead. During an expansion, consumer confidence is generally high as the job market is generally strong and many investments will have reached new highs. The consumer confidence report is usually released the last week of every month.

6.) **Durable Goods:** Durable goods can be described as items with a life expectancy of at least three years. Durable goods would include washers, dryers, stoves, computers, and other long lasting items. The report measures the level of shipments, inventories, and orders to manufacturers, not retailers. Durable good sales are generally up in an expanding economy and down in times of downturn and recession. This report is officially titled the Advance Report on Durable Goods Manufacturers' Shipments, Inventories, and Orders and is also released monthly, approximately three weeks after the reporting month ends.

7.) **ISM Manufacturing:** The health of the manufacturing sector is vitally important to the U.S. economy since approximately 10% of the nation's workforce works in manufacturing. The report is officially titled The ISM Manufacturing Report on Business and is released on the first business day of the month. An index level over 50 indicates growth. Although its contribution to the economy has been on a steady decline over the last several decades, the manufacturing sector, in 2012, made up approximately 12% of the nation's GDP and had the highest multiplier effect of any sector. For every $1 spent in manufacturing, almost another $1.50 was added to the economy. To complete the report, a survey is sent to 300 purchasing managers asking about the level of new orders, production, employment, supplier deliveries, and inventories.

8.) **Housing Starts:** The housing starts report details the number of single and multifamily homes being built. As we all know, when a home is built and then purchased, it calls for further spending on appliances, fixtures, and other household related goods. This report gives us a pretty solid indication of where the economy is going approximately three to six months ahead of time. The housing starts report, which is officially titled New Residential Construction, is released monthly around the middle of the month and is heavily watched by Wall Street.

9.) **Existing Home Sales:** The Existing Home Sales report is released monthly by the National Association of Realtors toward the end of every month. This report measures the number of existing home sales that have been completed and closed. This report is a good source of information when looking to examine the health of the real estate market as the president of the NAR and its chief economists will often outline the condition of the sector and mention any headwinds that it may be facing.

10.) **S&P/Case-Shiller Home Price Index:** The Case-Shiller Home Price Index is the last indicator that I will briefly discuss. It is also released monthly on the last Tuesday of the month, but it reports data from two months prior. The Case-Shiller Home Price Index measures the increase or decrease in residential home prices. It has both a 10-city index and a 20-city index, and it reports on metropolitan cities. This report probably, in my opinion, provides the best reading on the direction of home prices, which are important for real estate investors and for the overall economy since rising home prices have a tendency to promote economic growth.

Supply & Demand

One of the most important, yet simple, aspects of economics is supply and demand. Generally, when the supply of something is high and the demand for it is low, the price for that item generally declines. When the supply of something is low and the demand for it is high, prices generally increase since there are more buyers than product available.

This situation is very evident in today's society. For example, when the demand for gas or housing goes up, the price usually goes up with it, especially if the demand increases in comparison with supply.

On the other hand, if the demand for something is low at Walmart or Target and the supply of that item is high, the item usually goes on clearance to entice shoppers to buy.

This also is the case when department stores have clearance sales to get rid of old trends or fashions that are no longer demanding the attention of consumers. An example of this would be in the fall season and summer clothes are marked down to their lowest prices. This is because the demand for summer clothes is very low in the fall and, therefore, retailers need extremely low prices to entice consumers.

The Federal Reserve

The Federal Reserve System, which was created by Congress in 1913, is the central bank for the United States. As the country's central bank, it acts as a bank for the government and for other banks. The Federal Reserve System is comprised of the Board of Governors, 12 regional Federal Reserve Banks, and a number of branches that are supervised by the Board of Governors.

The Federal Reserve Board of Governors has seven members, who are appointed by the president and confirmed by the Senate. Board members serve terms of 14 years, which are staggered; therefore, a member's term shall expire every even-numbered year. After serving a full term, Board members may not be reappointed; however, if a Board member is appointed and confirmed to finish the term of a resigning member, he or she may later be appointed to a full term. The chairman and vice chairman of the Board serve four-year terms and may be reappointed after their terms expire as long as they are still Board members.

The two most important duties of the Federal Reserve System are creating and implementing the nation's monetary policy and supervising and regulating banks. The most significant goals of monetary policy are to ensure both price stability and full employment. On the other end of the spectrum, setting reserve requirements, which determine how much banks can lend, is the most important duty in its role as bank supervisor.

Federal Open Market Committee

The Federal Open Market Committee, which is a part of the Federal Reserve System, is responsible for setting monetary policy and consists of the seven-member Board of Governors, the president of the Federal Reserve Bank of New York, and four of the remaining 11 Reserve Bank presidents, who serve on a rotating schedule; therefore, there are 12 members on this committee at all times. The Board of Governors and the New York Reserve Bank president always serve on the Federal Open Market Committee. The 11 Reserve Bank presidents who rotate serve one-year terms on the committee.

It is important to note that all of the Reserve Bank presidents are allowed to attend committee meetings and participate in discussions; however, only five in any given year are allowed to vote. Committee membership changes at the first regularly scheduled meeting of the year.

The Federal Open Market Committee holds eight regularly scheduled meetings each year in Washington, D.C. During these meetings, there is generally a discussion on the state of the economy and a vote is taken whether or not to change its target for the federal funds rate.

Federal Funds Rate

Banks are required to maintain a certain level of funds (or reserves) that cannot be loaned out to borrowers. Such reserves can be kept in vault or with Federal Reserve Banks. The Board of Governors (and not the Federal Open Market Committee) has sole control over setting reserve requirements. When a bank becomes in danger of not being in compliance with the required reserve amount, it can take a loan from the Federal Reserve or from another bank.

The federal funds rate is the interest rate that banks charge each other for overnight loans. The actual rate at which banks charge each other is negotiated between the two banks, and the Federal Reserve has only limited control over this key rate. The Federal Open Market Committee also uses its ability to buy and sell government and, more recently, mortgage-backed securities to affect interest rates.

When the Federal Open Market Committee wishes to slow down economic activity, it will take action to raise interest rates and decrease the nation's money supply. This, in turn, discourages banks from placing themselves in a position to need to borrow money and will cause them to loan out less to bank customers. When the Federal Open Market Committee wishes to stimulate economic activity, it will take action to lower interest rates and increase the nation's money supply. This, in turn, encourages banks to lend more, which leads to increased spending by consumers and businesses alike.

Discount Rate

The discount rate, which is ultimately controlled by the Board of Governors, is the interest rate that the Federal Reserve charges banks for short-term loans. Although not currently, the discount rate is usually set at approximately 1 percentage point above the federal funds rate. Since banks can procure loans from other banks at the federal funds rate, a loan from the Federal Reserve at the discount rate is basically a tool of last resort for banking institutions seeking to raise short-term capital.

Key Federal Reserve Reports

There are several Federal Reserve reports that are followed closely by investors and business leaders, and they are the Beige Book, FOMC meeting statement, and the FOMC meeting minutes.

Beige Book

The Beige Book contains an up-to-date report on the economy that is collected by the 12 Federal District Banks, who collect information from business leaders in their respective regions. The information is compiled and distributed to members of the Federal Reserve and to the public two weeks prior to the next FOMC meeting. This information is then used to help shape debate for any action pertaining to monetary policy.

FOMC Meeting Statement

The meeting statement is the actual decision of the FOMC on its target for the federal funds rate. The report is released shortly after the FOMC meeting and can often have an impact on the stock and bond markets.

FOMC Meeting Minutes

The meeting minutes are notes from the actual discussion and debate that determined the direction of the federal funds rate. The meeting minutes provide great detail as to why the FOMC made its policy decision. This report is released three weeks after the FOMC meeting, so there are many investors who believe that this report is untimely and mostly ineffective as a tool for trading or investing.

Last Words

Having your finger on the pulse of the economy is critical if you are going to have long-term success with investing or if you plan on having a successful business operation.

Generally, in times of a bad market or downturn, most businesses decrease their spending and tighten their belts as much as possible. As stated by Robert Kiyosaki, during times of a bad economy, I think that extra spending should be done on advertising and other marketing to give your business or product as much exposure as possible.

When investing, it is unwise to buy real estate or stocks at inflated prices during the high points of an expansion or peak in the economy, but without the proper education, one can't possible know what is considered a good or bad time in the economy.

On the other hand, I recommend buying underpriced real estate and stocks during bad times and holding them until the market recovers. During the hard times in the economy, people are often scared and make decisions based on that emotion and sell very good investments for much less than they are worth.

Likewise, when the economy is strong, people are more than willing to buy overinflated investments because they always think it can only get better, forgetting the last recession that took place only a few years earlier. It was Warren Buffett who said it best, "Be fearful when others are greedy and greedy when others are fearful."

Chapter 3

Real Estate Investing: The Basics & Beyond

In the world of investing, there are practically hundreds, if not thousands, of different investment options for an investor to choose from. Often, many people are advised that the best investment choices are in various stocks or mutual funds. Although it can be true at times, such as during a credit crunch, it is typically not the case.

Generally, when you question someone who makes this type of statement, he will tell you how stocks have grown, on average, approximately 10% annually over the last 75 years and so on and so forth. In many cases, investing in stocks can be a good decision to help add diversity to your portfolio, but in no way should it be the main piece of your investment puzzle during an economic climate with normal credit conditions. The reason why stocks shouldn't be the center of your portfolio is the huge benefit that you get from investing in real estate called leverage.

Before I begin discussing the wealth strategies for real estate investing, I must advise you that some of the scenarios that are written between chapters three and four regarding real estate financing are based on a normal, free-flowing credit environment. As you may be aware, due to the real estate bubble burst and subsequent credit crunch, we have not had a normal, free-flowing credit environment since the start of the financial crisis and may not see one again in the near future.

Although I don't believe that the mortgage industry will return to identical operations as before the Great Recession, I do predict that once the economy and our nation's employment situation return close to full strength, credit will again be easy to obtain, including mortgage loans.

As of the end 2013, 100% financing is very hard to come by. Unless you qualify for a VA loan, it can be almost impossible to qualify for 100% financing. The closest thing to 100% financing that a first-time homebuyer can expect in today's economy is an F.H.A. loan, which only requires a 3.5% down payment as long as the borrower has a credit score above 580 and can find a lender that is willing to make the loan. F.H.A. borrowers with credit scores between 500 and 579 are required to have down payments of 10% and are also faced with the task of finding a willing lender.

Real Property and Personal Property

Property can be divided between real property and personal property. Real property is land and anything permanently attached to it, such as trees, buildings, and anything permanently attached to the building. Personal property would be items such as clothes, jewelry, kitchen tables, and anything else that's not directly or indirectly permanently attached to land.

The good thing about real estate is that you can touch it. If you have the address, you can drive by and see what type of condition the property is in without having to be a real estate genius. On the other hand, if you are not literate in advanced finance concepts, trying to figure out if a company is in good shape can be almost impossible.

Banks understand this very well, and this is one of the main reasons why they won't hesitate to give someone with a good credit and employment background all of the money that he needs for a real estate investment. However, they would look at the same

A-credit borrower like he has lost his mind if he came in asking for a loan of any size to buy stocks.

This isn't meant to be a bashing of stocks because, like I said, stocks can be a very valuable piece to a solid portfolio. My purpose here is to separate the two and show the large difference in benefits between them. Investing in real estate has an enormous advantage over investing in publicly traded stocks, and I feel this is one of the many things that you must know about real estate.

Buying Your First Home: The Basics

Buying your first home can be a very challenging and mentally draining experience. This is, of course, if you aren't aware ahead of time of everything that is required of you and everything that you will be forced to go through in order to complete the process.

However, it is an experience that you should be happy to go through. It is one of the best ways to build wealth in this country, as the net worth of a homeowner is usually much higher than someone who is not a homeowner.

This is because when a home increases in value as it usually does in healthy real estate markets, it creates equity for the homeowner. Equity is the difference between what the home is worth and what you owe the mortgage lender. For example, let's say that you have a home that is now worth $200,000 and you owe the mortgage lender $150,000. The $50,000 difference between the $200,000 that it's worth and $150,000 that you owe is considered equity, and that equity is your portion of real ownership in the home.

When a person sells a home, after the mortgage lender and all fees are paid, the remaining money goes to the seller of the home, and it doesn't need to be shared with anyone, not even the bank that may have loaned him 95% of the money to purchase the property.

Generally, in any business agreement, when someone provides the start-up money of any amount, it is generally expected for that investor to receive a percentage of the profits. However, in real estate there is no such expectation. When all things are considered, I firmly believe that real estate is the best investment out there for the individual investor who has a strong credit background.

Before you start looking to buy your first home, it is important to make sure that your credit is intact. The better your credit, the lower the interest rate will be that you will qualify for, so this is very important as it can save you tens of thousands of dollars over the life of the loan.

This doesn't mean that you must have perfect credit. It just means that you should make sure that during the last 12 to 24 months leading up to your home purchase that you don't have any 30-day late payments on any of your lines of credit that appear on your credit report.

If a person is late by 10 or 15 days on a credit account, it doesn't usually hurt his credit report as your report only shows blemishes for payments that are not paid at all or for those that were paid greater than 30 days late.

Lines of credit that generally report monthly to the credit bureaus include mortgages, car loans, credit cards, and student loans. Generally, the electric, gas, and water companies do not report to the credit agencies unless you become so delinquent that your account is sent to collections, which also isn't good if you are looking to buy a house soon.

Once you've done a good job of securing a good credit profile, it is wise to start shopping for the best mortgage lender for your situation. It is important to know that all lenders are not created equal; therefore, it is important to do your due diligence and find the best one for your particular situation. One lender may have a better program for perfect credit, while another may have the best program for fair or good credit.

In the process of shopping for a loan, it is important to know your credit score ahead of time, so when companies give you quotes, they don't have to pull your credit, which can knock your score down a few points.

Once you find a lender that you are comfortable with, you should ask to be pre-approved so that you can know how much of a home you can actually afford. After you get pre-approved, you should then find a good realtor in your local area.

It is very important **not** to find a realtor before you find a lender because many realtors are notorious for referring you to their business sharing mortgage buddy down the street, which may not be in your best interest.

In my opinion, at least 50% of all realtors have a mortgage lender whom they trade business with even if they know that the homebuyer could get a much better deal elsewhere. In return, realtors expect their mortgage buddies to refer to them all business that goes to them first, which isn't as bad because you as the homebuyer won't pay the realtor anyway.

Your realtor is paid from the commission that the seller agreed to pay his realtor when he listed his home for sale. If your agent brings you, as a buyer, to the seller, the commission that would have went solely to the selling agent is now split between the two agents 50/50 unless some other agreement has been worked out.

The average selling realtor's commission ranges from 5 to 8 percent depending on how good the realtor is and how hard he or she believes it will be to sell the home. To give you an example of how this works, let's say a realtor's commission is 6% and the selling price is $200,000. The total commission for selling this house would be $12,000. If two agents are involved (buyer's agent and seller's agent), the $12,000 commission would be split between the two agents 50/50, each agent getting $6,000 in commission.

Once you find a good realtor that you are comfortable with, you can start looking for a home. It is of the essence that you like the realtor that you choose as you will be spending a lot of time with him or her riding around looking at houses. In many cases, your realtor will become your temporary best friend as you will begin to see him or her day and night with phone conversations and emails seeming routine until you find your home.

While looking at various homes, it is a good idea to visit the area at different times during the day to get a good feel for the true identity of the neighborhood. While visiting the neighborhood, it is always a good idea to knock on doors and ask questions about the neighborhood. From my past experiences, most of the elderly neighbors will be more than willing to tell you everything that they know about the neighborhood, which will generally be some very helpful information for you and help you to decide if that is an area where you really want to live.

Once you find a home that you are interested in, you and your realtor will then prepare an offer for the home. Most offers are made with several common contingencies to protect the potential buyer: contingent upon financing, appraisal exceeding the purchase price, and inspection being approved by the buyer within 10 days after inspection.

In many cases, a realtor will have the inside scoop on what the bottom line is that the seller is willing to accept for the home. Realtors usually get this information from the seller's agent as they will both do all that they can to work together and sell the home.

This can be seen as very disloyal as a seller is under the impression that everything that he discusses in secrecy with his agent is kept confidential between the two of them. This is generally not the case as both agents will share information with each other. This information ranges from the seller's agent telling the bottom line that the seller will accept for the home to the buyer's agent sharing the maximum dollar amount that the buyer is willing to pay for a particular property.

With that said, please don't expect anyone in a real estate transaction to be entirely on your side, not even yourself. If a person doesn't have his emotions in check before going into a real estate transaction, his emotions will normally influence the buying decision, which may lead a logical person to make an emotion based, irrational decision.

When making an offer on a home, it is best to offer slightly under the amount that your realtor has told you is the seller's bottom line, while at the same time asking the seller to pay some of your closing costs.

For example, if the listing price is $265,000 and your realtor told you that the seller's bottom line is $240,000, you should offer $230,000 with the seller paying $6,900 of your closing costs.

In many cases, the seller will accept this offer as it is close to what he wanted and his realtor will put a little pressure on him to do so. At this point, the seller will accept, reject, or make a counter-offer.

If the seller rejects your offer, you can make another offer closer to what he is asking for the home in hopes that he will accept. If the seller makes a counter-offer, he will generally ask for more money and, in most cases, the two parties will find a way to meet in the middle.

In any case, once you have a purchase and sell agreement is when the ball starts rolling. At this point, you would order an inspection and then approve or disapprove what the report reveals. Generally, no inspection report shows a perfect property, and whatever flaws are found can be used to your advantage to negotiate a lower price on the home.

After all of the final kinks are worked out with the inspection report, you then contact your mortgage lender and let it know that you have a purchase and sell agreement on a home. At this time, you would complete an application in person, online, or over the phone and lock in your interest rate and closing costs.

You will then need to send in verification of pay stubs, bank statements, and potentially any other income or asset verification needed. You will also be required to sign some mortgage disclosures that include a Good Faith Estimate (GFE) and a Truth in Lending Statement.

After all of this information is received by the lender, it will generally order the appraisal for your home. The appraiser will do research on similar homes that have sold in the area of the home that you're buying and examine the home to come up with an approximate value of the property.

This process usually goes smoothly, but in some cases you may find out that the seller is overcharging for the home and the appraised value may come back less than what the seller is willing to sell it for. In most situations, the lender will not be willing to fund the loan in this type of situation.

If the seller is not willing to renegotiate, it is usually a deal breaker. In most cases, however, sellers are reasonable and will do what they need to do to sell the home.

Simultaneously, when the appraisal is ordered, the mortgage company will order your title work to make sure that the seller is the actual legal owner of the home and that there are no defects in title that materially affect the value of the property. Also, the mortgage company will do an employment verification to make sure that you're actively employed as you stated in your application.

If all of this information comes back fine, your file will be submitted for underwriting. The underwriter will double check everything in the file and give a last say of yes, no, or yes upon certain conditions. A common condition may be that the buyer has to pay off certain collection accounts before closing. Whatever the case, after final approval from the underwriter, the file is sent to the closing department and the date of your closing is scheduled.

One of the last things that you must perform before closing is setting up your homeowners insurance. Generally, you will have to pay one year worth of insurance with your insurance company, which usually will cost between $600 and $2,500, depending on the size, value, and location of the home.

One thing I highly recommend is using the same company that you have your car insurance with, as your agent will normally give you a significant discount on both for doing so.

The closing is the final stage in the home buying process and can sometimes be the most mentally draining and demanding. At closing, you will often meet the sellers of the home unless they signed ahead of time. This is also where you literally get to read and sign dozens of forms.

It is very important to make sure that the interest rate and closing costs that you agreed to with your mortgage lender are what you are signing for at closing. It is very normal for the lender to offer you a good rate and low closing costs in order to win your business and then switch them both on you at closing.

If this happens to you, I recommend walking away from the closing table without signing anything. This is what the mortgage industry calls the "bait and switch." Don't go for it as this is very unethical and deserves to be walked away from.

On the other hand, if everything is as agreed to, you will literally spend hours reviewing and signing papers before finally being handed keys to your new home. At this point, you are now considered a homeowner and can begin receiving the benefits of homeownership.

Although this may have been a long, tiring process, it is definitely worth it. Once you go to your new home, it is always good to introduce yourself to all of your new neighbors, especially those that are right next to you.

Investing in Real Estate

As stated before, real estate is a great investment. No other investment out there has the benefits of real estate or even comes close for that matter. There are many ways to begin a career investing in real estate, and there are many different types of properties that a person can choose for investment.

The most common investment is in residential real estate. Generally, when a person takes this route, he buys single-family or two-family homes to begin with and then moves up as his experience or financial situation gets better.

The best way to show you how this works is to illustrate a scenario of a person who begins a career investing in real estate. I will walk you through as she moves from one property to the next, using some very good techniques to get the absolute best mortgage possible.

The story that I'm going to walk you through is the story of a woman named Michelle. When Michelle graduated from Emory University in Atlanta, GA, with a double major in business and communications, she immediately got a job at a large Fortune 500 company as the assistant sales director.

Her new job came with a comfortable salary of $50,000 and a chance for a yearly bonus of up to $25,000. Being a hard worker for Michelle was inherent, so she knew that she could motivate her team to the highest level possible.

After saving money to build a security nest for six months, she purchased her first home that had three bedrooms, two bathrooms, and a two-car garage, 10 minutes from downtown Atlanta for $135,000. She was qualified for an F.H.A. loan, which only required a 3.5% down payment, since she was a first-time homebuyer and intended to owner occupy the home.

Her total PITI (principal, interest, taxes, and insurance) payment was only $1,025, which left her with plenty of extra cash each month to save for her next investment. Although she liked this home a lot, she didn't plan on living in it for long and she wanted to turn it into an investment property and move up to a slightly bigger house.

After a year of living in her first home, Michelle hired a real estate agent to help her find her next home to buy that she was going to live in. Her realtor advised her that the best way to turn her current home into an investment property would be to hire a reputable property management company.

The realtor informed Michelle that for a small percentage of rents collected that the property management company would collect rents, pay any bills related to the property, handle any evictions if needed, and schedule all maintenance and repairs. She thought that this was a good idea as she assumed that the downside to investing in real estate was going to be receiving calls at 3:00 a.m. about the hot water heater not working.

Using a property management company erased that concern and increased Michelle's chances of collecting rent on time each month as tenants are more likely to pay a company on time than they are a person (the homeowner) that they might not even like.

After hiring a property management company to take care of the property, she focused solely on finding her next home that would ultimately become an investment one day.

After looking for about three weeks, Michelle had a purchase and sale agreement on a nice home about 15 minutes from downtown Atlanta for $155,000. The home had three bedrooms, three bathrooms, and a two-car garage, very similar to her first home. In addition to the three normal conditions in the contract (conditioned upon financing, appraisal, and inspection), she also added a condition that stated that her current home needed to be rented out with a one-year lease before closing. This covered her end as she didn't want to be stuck paying for two mortgages.

She hired a very good property management company that was able to rent out her current home approximately three weeks before closing on her new home. The rent being charged for her home was $1,150, which was enough to cover PITI and the 8% charge to cover property management fees, so she was in pretty good shape to move forward.

After she closed on her new home, she became very excited about how the real estate business worked and made a commitment to find her next home within a year from the day of closing on her second home.

Less than a year after moving into her new home, she hired her current property management company to find a tenant for her current home as she was ready to make her next move up and buy her third property.

Before Michelle had a chance to call the realtor, the property management company already had a qualified tenant who was ready to move in within 30 days. This caused Michelle and her agent to speed things up and look for that next property with extreme urgency.

Due to working with Michelle on her two prior home purchases, her realtor had a good idea of what type of home she wanted and they found their next home in seven days. Purchasing this home didn't go as smoothly as the other two as her mortgage guy told her that her debt-to-income ratio was getting too high and that she would have to keep the mortgage under $140,000.

This is where the second problem came in at. The mortgage lender told Michelle that by her buying a property that was worth less than her current home, the underwriter would automatically assume that this was an investment property as there was no good, logical reason for her to step down in home size except for one.

Her mortgage lender told her that the only logical excuse that the underwriter was likely to accept was that the third home that she was going to buy was going to be closer to her employer than her current home.

So this meant that Michelle would be forced to buy a home that was closer to her job than her current home was or she would be forced to get the mortgage based on an investment property that would have a much higher interest rate, higher closing costs, and a higher down payment requirement. She didn't want to pay investment property rates and did the smart thing and found a home that was about 10 minutes closer to her employer than her current home was.

After she bought her third home, she decided to put a hold to her real estate purchases and wanted to grow some equity in her current homes so that she could sell and move on to bigger and better investments.

She waited for about two years watching her property values dramatically increase. Purchasing homes so close to downtown really paid off. After two years, her first home that she purchased for $135,000 was now worth $180,000. The second home that she bought for $155,000 was now worth $200,000, and the third home that she purchased for $140,000 was now worth $190,000.

Altogether she had over $140,000 worth of equity combined in her three homes. She decided to sell all three homes with the same realtor that she had purchased the homes with, who in return gave her a discount and sold her homes for her at a partial rate of 4%.

Due to the areas being as hot as they were, all three homes sold within four months and gave Michelle over $110,000 after all fees and closing costs were paid. At each closing, Michelle's smile became bigger and bigger as she knew that she was headed toward financial security.

Before she completed the sale and closing of her last home, she had a nice home with four bedrooms, three bathrooms, and a three-car garage under contract for $300,000 that had a mortgage payment of just under $2,000 when combined with taxes and insurance.

She bought this home with a down payment of only 10% and with plans of living in it for a while as she now wanted to focus on larger residential real estate, specifically small to mid-size apartment buildings.

She first tried to get pre-approved for a commercial loan with her current loan officer, but he informed her that his company couldn't finance any buildings over four units and recommended her to a good commercial lender that he knew and previously shared business with.

Michelle had over $200,000 at the time she met with the commercial lender, who was very impressed with Michelle's ability to build such a large nest egg only a few years after college.

After reviewing her credit and verifying her employment, the lender approved Michelle for a $500,000 commercial loan as long as she put down a minimum of 20% of her own money at closing.

The lender then referred her to a good commercial real estate agent that he shared business with. The lender assured Michelle that the realtor would be able to get her top quality for her money, which he was correct about.

The first building that the realtor showed Michelle was a 20-unit apartment building 10 minutes from downtown Atlanta. The building was appraised at over $600,000, but the realtor knew the selling realtor and got the word on it before it officially became a listing.

The seller was willing to accept $525,000 for the property as long as Michelle could get financing lined up and close within 45 days. To his surprise, Michelle was already ahead of the game and had a pre-approval letter in her back pocket.

Michelle made a formal offer in writing for $525,000, and the seller gladly accepted. Three days after they came to an agreement on the sale price, Michelle did the wise thing and had the property inspected. This was very expensive as the building had 20 units, but it was well worth the cost.

During the inspection, the inspector discovered several problems with the plumbing and electricity in several units and estimated the repair to cost over $15,000. After hearing this news, Michelle got excited as she knew that she could use this information to her advantage. After discussing her concerns of the inspection with the seller, she was able to do a final negotiation on the price and ended up getting the building for $490,000.

While signing her share of paperwork at the closing table, Michelle couldn't stop smiling as she saw her net worth increase by over $100,000 in a matter of hours. This was a big move for her as the building brought in an average of $600 per unit for a total gross income of $12,000. Her mortgage on the property was less than $4,500 and, after all expenses were paid, gave her a net monthly profit of slightly over $6,000.

She then used this income to pay for her current mortgage on the home that she was living in and to cover the lease for her Mercedes Benz, which had a monthly payment of $800.

The income that she was receiving from her apartment building gave her more than enough income to support a very comfortable lifestyle, not including the solid income that she was getting with her current employer. At this point, she was basically living off of assets and enjoying herself while doing so.

Although Michelle put herself in a very good position financially, she wasn't close to being satisfied and she went on to purchase three more apartment buildings in less than two years. With rental income and steady promotions at work, her financial situation became very comfortable and she was able to quit her job and attend graduate school at Cornell University in New York.

She was studying to get her MBA in Hotel Management as she wanted her next step to be in hotel ownership. She knew that in two years when she graduated that she would be able to sell some of her apartment buildings for very nice profits, which could potentially work as a great down payment on a mid-level hotel.

While in school, Michelle was given the opportunity to work several internships at very reputable hotel franchises, which gave her first-hand experience in the hotel business. Since Michelle had a very nice income from her investments that she made back home, she didn't have to work and so she spent all of her time in graduate school studying and learning all that she could about the hotel business.

After graduating with her MBA in Hotel Management from one of the top hospitality schools in the country, she was on a mission to take the Atlanta hotel scene by storm and she sold three of her apartment buildings for a profit of $575,000. With the financial condition that she was in, as well as her internationally respected MBA from Cornell in Hotel Management, Michelle had no problem getting approved for a $4,000,000 loan to purchase a very nice hotel.

The hotel that Michelle ended up buying was about five minutes from downtown Atlanta and had annual net profits of over $600,000. The price of the hotel was $3.7 million and required Michelle to put down 25%, which was approximately $925,000 plus some costs to pay her broker in the transaction.

Although the income from her hotel was enough to live a very extravagant lifestyle, she maintained a very nice, modest living, only using revenue from the remaining apartment building.

She kept this up for three years accumulating over $2,000,000 in liquid assets. Of course, not being one to settle for less, Michelle purchased a second hotel about 20 minutes from downtown. This time she stepped it up a little and made the purchase at $7,000,000. She put 25% down once again, which was approximately $1,750,000. This time it was well worth it as the hotel had annual net profits of almost $2.25 million.

With an income of approximately $3 million annually, she decided that it was time to sell her last apartment building, which she sold for a profit of $300,000. Life was great for Michelle and she went on to buy two more hotels within a three-year period and raised her total income to over $7 million annually. She also managed to grow her net worth to over $40 million before her 35th birthday. Michelle is just one example of how someone can gain a life of riches in the world of real estate investing when focused and determined.

Real Estate Investing in All Climates

During a downturn, trough, recovery, expansion, or peak, a great real estate investment can be found and profited from. Real estate can be a good investment no matter the season for several reasons, but there are two in particular that I would like to cover:

1.) **Foreclosures on Adjustable Rate Mortgages**: Due to a never ending list of foreclosures, there are always under-priced homes on the market that must sell, in many cases, for approximately half of the appraised value. With the large use of ARMs (adjustable rate mortgages), more people than ever are falling victim to foreclosure as they are not able to refinance and can no longer make their mortgage payments once they adjust.

Not having good sight or vision for the future, they ignored the form at closing that stated that their interest rates could jump as high as 9.75% at the first adjustment period and another 1% annually until their interest rates reached a cap of 13%.

This, of course, made a very large difference when the payment adjusted and became almost twice as high as it was originally. In some cases, this causes the sellers to be put in a position to sell or be foreclosed upon and, with the credit effects of a foreclosure being close to deadly, a credit savvy homeowner will do almost anything to avoid foreclosure.

2.) **You Don't Have to Pay the Mortgage**: One of my favorite aspects of a good real estate investment is that the owner of the investment is rarely the one that ends up making the monthly mortgage payments. Generally, the mortgage and all other related expenses are paid by the tenants of the property by way of rents collected by the owner or the property management company. Even in a situation where properties aren't appreciating at a fast pace, an investor can still enjoy the benefits of equity by way of timely monthly payments from the tenants.

Spotting Good Investments

Spotting a good real estate investment can be a simple, yet challenging, task. Depending on a person's investment philosophy, a good investment can be determined by many different things.

In my opinion, a property that has the potential to increase in value steadily over a three to five-year period as well as having a strong enough rental market in order for a tenant to cover all related expenses for the property is a good one. Of course it has to fit within each individual investor's investment goals, but generally this is enough for a property to get my time and attention.

To make sure a property meets these qualifications, it is important to do a cash-flow analysis that adds all income from the property and subtracts all related expenses, which should include possible maintenance fees.

If after completing the required math your gut still tells you that the subject property may make a good one, it is a good idea to do more due diligence and look at the history of home sales in the area to see how fast they have been appreciating over the last three to five years.

When looking at these numbers, it is important to remember that home values generally increase a lot faster in markets of low interest rates and easy credit since the demand for homes is a lot higher when mortgage interest rates are low and credit is easy to obtain.

Real Estate Investment Trusts

I think real estate investment trusts are great tools for investors to gain exposure to the real estate market, especially for investors who have damaged credit profiles. Many REITs are public companies that can be categorized as real estate stocks that invest in commercial real estate, such as office buildings, shopping malls, hotels, and apartment buildings. They have been very attractive over the last four years (2009-2012) as REITs have handsomely outgained the S&P 500 during that time span. REITs also pay much higher dividend yields than most companies listed in the S&P 500.

1031 Tax-Deferred Exchange

The 1031 tax-deferred exchange is one of the best ideas that the government ever came up with in regard to doing something helpful for real estate investors. If used properly, the 1031 exchange law can help a real estate investor become very rich in a much shorter time.

The 1031 tax-deferred exchange gives an investor the opportunity to sell a piece of property and put the total proceeds from the sale into another property without having to pay taxes on the gain or profit before doing so.

There are several guidelines that must be adhered to in order to make this a success, and they are listed below.

1.) The properties must be a "like-kind" exchange. This means that the property sold and the new property that is being purchased must be similar to one another in reference to their character. For example, a home that was held for investment can only be exchanged for other real property that is for investment. This could mean a single-family home being traded for another single-family home or a single-family home being traded for a 20-unit apartment building. As long as the properties have like-kind character, the 1031 exchange can be applied. It is important to note that property used primarily for personal use does not apply.

2.) A new property must be identified within 45 days of the sale of the investment where the profits have come from.

3.) The trade or exchange must take place and close within 180 days of the sale of the investment where the profits have come from.

4.) The proceeds must be held at a qualified intermediary, such as a title company or bank that can act as an exchange bank. This means that you can't just deposit this money at your regular local bank without it acting as an exchange bank, and you definitely can't take the money home with you.

5.) The property must be held for a long enough period of time for it to appear that the intent of the acquisition was for investment and not to just immediately sell for a profit. Deciding if this requirement has been fulfilled is basically done on a case-by-case basis, but typically a year is sufficient.

To give you a clear illustration of how the 1031 tax-deferred exchange works, I'll give you the story of Jessica. Jessica had a Master of Science in Psychology, which she earned in less than two years after completing her four-year degree in business.

She had a lot on her side and she was determined to add wealth to the picture. She had a high paying job with a large oil company, but she was ready to live off of assets and spend her weekdays in the manner that she chose and work when she pleased.

After years of saving money, she purchased a small 10-unit apartment building for $300,000. Although she enjoyed the income that came in from the building on a monthly basis, she was ready to sell after two years as the property's value increased from $300,000 to $525,000.

After selling the property, Jessica had net proceeds of over $200,000, which she held at her local title company with the intention to purchase a like-kind property.

After two weeks (within the 45-day requirement), Jessica spotted a 20-unit apartment building that was selling for $750,000 and notified the title company that she had a property in mind.

After searching for another couple of weeks to see if she could find anything else that she wanted to invest the money in (the proceeds for a 1031 exchange can go into more than one property as long as they are all like-kind), she decided that she was going to put the entire $200,000 into her new building and closed within 75 days (within the 180-day requirement).

In this case, since Jessica used the 1031 exchange to perfection, she was able to avoid paying taxes on the profit that she had gained from the sale of her original apartment building, which allowed her to put more money into a larger investment.

After holding this apartment building for three years, Jessica was again ready to sell as the value rose from $750,000 to $1.3 million. In this case, she was able to sell the property and gain a profit of over $550,000, which she again held at her local title company with the intention of buying a like-kind property.

This time around, she found two properties that she wanted to invest in. Being allowed to do so, she invested half of the money into an upscale 18-unit building and the other half into a large 30-unit apartment building.

One important thing to note when exchanging properties is that you do eventually have to pay taxes at the end of the line when you finally sell a property and want to take some cash out and use it in a different way other than to purchase a like-kind property.

Watching Jessica utilize her total profits to invest in like-kind properties should give a good picture of how it works and another idea on how you can make it a success for you.

Tax Benefits of Depreciation

Another great benefit with investing in real estate is the tax favor real estate investors receive. Although most homes, in healthy real estate markets, don't depreciate in value, a real estate investor is allowed to depreciate a residential investment property over 27.5 years (39 years for commercial property). This is a great benefit and usually makes most of the income received tax-free.

Depreciation is considered an expense that is deducted from the income that's received. For example, if an investment property had $3,000 worth of income and $3,000 worth of depreciation, the taxable income would be $0.

Depreciation is calculated by dividing the purchase price (plus acquisition cost, such as legal fees and title insurance) of the investment property (minus the value of the land, as land can't be depreciated) by 27.5. For example, if an investment property (minus the land) costs $300,000, you would divide that by 27.5. That would give you $10,909 of depreciation that can be subtracted annually from the income for the property. If the net income is less than $10,909, the income received on this property would be basically tax-free.

This is a great benefit. The only slight downside is that this decreases your cost basis by the amount that it was depreciated by. This means that it creates a larger profit at the time of sale, but if using the 1031 exchange, this downside is basically irrelevant.

Using Property Management Companies

A good property management company can be a real estate investor's best friend and, in some cases, can also be his worst enemy. A good property management company will fill any vacancies, collect all rents, mail your mortgage payments, execute evictions, and schedule any maintenance work that is required for the preservation of the property.

A good property management company will do extensive credit and background checks before putting someone into your property and will be very firm, yet professional and respectful, about collecting rents on a timely basis.

A good property management company will save an investor from a million and one headaches, as the investor rarely, if ever, comes into contact with the tenants. This means that if the hot water heater breaks down, instead of calling you, the tenant will call the property manager. Depending on the level of business that you give a property management company, it will generally charge a management fee of 5 to 8 percent of the rents collected. It will also generally charge a fee for finding tenants that can range from a couple hundred dollars to as much as the first month's rent.

I find property management companies very useful, but one must be careful of unscrupulous property management companies that will steal from you, so it is important to make sure that your property manager sends you a monthly statement and that you review it and question any discrepancies.

Flipping Real Estate

Although flipping real estate is probably considered more to be gambling than investing, I thought that some of my readers would want me to cover it, so I'll touch on the basics of the matter.

Flipping real estate involves purchasing a property for a low price and then quickly reselling the property at a profit. Sometimes the property is assigned to a third party without the title ever being put into the investor's hands. Flipping can be done in many ways, and I'll cover a couple to wrap up this chapter on real estate investing.

The two tactics that I'm going to cover are an outright purchase and then sell, and the other will be assigning a contract to a third party without ever taking possession of the property.

Purchase & Then Sell

This is probably the most common form of flip since many houses are rehabbed first before being put back on the market to be sold. This is almost impossible when assigning a contract and very risky as well. To give you a clear illustration of how this form of flipping would take place, I'll give you the story of Mya.

Mya was looking for some fast income and was informed about the possible benefits of flipping real estate from a friend of hers. Under his direction, she had some signs made with statements such as "We Buy Homes Fast" and "Avoid Foreclosure."

The first day that the signs were up, she got about 15 calls. Not all of the calls were quality as many people wanted full value for their homes, which would have left no room to profit for Mya if she had bought a home at full price.

Eventually, Mya got a call from a desperate seller who had lost her employment with a prestigious accounting firm and needed to sell badly in order to avoid foreclosure. During the first two minutes of the phone call, Mya wisely found out that the home was worth $180,000, the lady owed $115,000, and she was willing to accept $125,000 for the property if Mya could purchase the home and close within 30 days.

Mya had excellent credit, so she was able to get financing and she purchased the property and closed within the 30-day time frame. The home was in a great area as it was located near some good schools and close to both shopping and highways.

Immediately, Mya had the interior painted and did some other minor work that cost her around $2,000. Not considering the down payment and closing costs, Mya had around $127,000 invested in the home. She didn't have much of any closing costs when she bought the home because she agreed to a low closing costs loan that came with a much higher interest rate. This was a good idea since she was only going to be keeping this home for a short period of time.

After having the work done, Mya had the home appraised and it came back at $190,000. She then put ads in the newspaper stating that she had a $190,000 property selling for only $160,000.

Within hours after the ads were posted, she received numerous phone calls from motivated buyers who began bidding on the home, and the high demand allowed Mya to actually sell the home for $168,000. Remember supply & demand? The demand was higher than the supply. This gave Mya a quick profit of approximately $40,000, which she was very excited about. However, she was slightly disappointed when she learned that she would not be able to use the 1031 exchange since she held the property for inventory and not for investment.

This was just a simple example of flipping real estate after taking the title in your name and can be used by anyone with a little ambition to become a successful real estate flipper (not investor).

There are a couple potential downfalls with using this approach. Many mortgage lenders will not finance a home if the seller has not held title for a certain period of time. In some cases, the lender wants the title to be in the seller's name for a minimum of 60 days, and some may require 90 days. Not all mortgage companies have this requirement, but it is important to know exactly who you're doing business with and to make sure the buyer of the home is willing to use a lender that doesn't have a title seasoning requirement.

Another potential downfall could be the value of the property decreasing before the seller has had enough time to sell at a profit. This generally will not happen if you buy the home with a large enough gap (value of home versus what you paid for it), which was the case with Mya, but it can still happen depending on many things, including the neighborhood or the condition of the economy.

If you buy a home at the peak of a business cycle when inflation is skyrocketing, this will cause the Federal Reserve (Federal Open Market Committee) to raise interest rates to control inflation, and property values will generally decline if unattractive interest rates appear on the market.

In some cases, if the demand for housing is much higher than the supply, high interest rates will not have as much of an impact on the value of homes since people still need a place to sleep.

Flipping real estate can be very lucrative if done correctly. It can also be very dangerous if done incorrectly, so be careful when choosing properties to flip.

Assigning Real Estate to a Third Party

Assigning real estate to a third party can either be an easy transaction or a nightmare in hell. For the most part, I like to consider most humans to be good-hearted people who spend most of their time trying to become successful and don't really have an interest in stopping the next man or woman from becoming successful. Sometimes, especially when flipping real estate, you learn that this is not always the case.

Surprisingly, when some people find out that you are about to make a quick profit from doing business with them, they look down at the situation. Even if their needs are being met in the transaction, some people have a problem with yours being met as if you are supposed to do business so that everyone else benefits except for you.

If you plan on assigning a real estate contract to someone, it is very important to notify everyone involved in writing from the beginning to help prevent any unnecessary lawsuits and legal headaches.

To now give you an illustration of flipping a property by assigning a contract, I'll give you the story of Kimberly. One day while driving home from work, Kimberly noticed a for sale sign on a beautiful two story home. She didn't have a chance at a mortgage because her credit was in drastic need of repair, so she knew that she couldn't flip the property by purchasing it outright since she couldn't get financing.

When she made the offer on the property, she listed the buyer of the home as herself or "assignee." She notified the seller that she was unlikely to be able to get approved for financing, which was a safe and ethical way out of the contract if needed.

Nevertheless, Kim was able to find a buyer that was willing to purchase the home for $10,000 more than Kim had it under contract for, which gave her a quick and easy $10,000 profit at closing.

Of course, Kim did the right thing and notified the new buyers immediately of what her plans were, and they were okay with it since they were able to get a home for 90% of its fair market value.

Last Words

Following the techniques and knowledge found in this chapter will put you in position to live very comfortably if that is what you desire; at the very least, you will be prepared to go through the battles of purchasing your first home.

Buying a home can be a mind-boggling task when unprepared, so I hope that you now feel that you can tackle this process with no problem. Also, if you never knew how to begin real estate investing, you should now know the basic steps to get started and possibly end up in a very good lifestyle supported by assets like Michelle.

Chapter 4

What You Need to Know About Mortgages

With all of the talk about real estate investing, it is important to note that it would not be possible, in most cases, without a mortgage loan. A mortgage is simply what you give the bank or lender for a loan for real property. The real property is generally the collateral for the loan.

In most cases, a person doesn't have the ability to buy a home or apartment building outright with cash and a loan is usually required to complete the transaction. Depending on the situation of the borrower, this may be an easy or difficult process.

A mortgage is definitely considered a secured loan, meaning that if the borrower defaults on the mortgage, the bank has the complete right and ability to foreclose on the home as a means for being paid back its capital.

Prime and Subprime

The mortgage loan that a person or family can usually qualify for is divided into two categories: prime and subprime. The difference between the two is usually tens or hundreds of thousands of dollars if both loans are held for the entire length of the loan.

The ideal situation of any potential homebuyer is to get his credit in order before buying a home so that he won't be faced with what some experts consider a predatory loan. However, many people will buy homes without first getting their credit situations in good shape and, therefore, will be forced to accept less than decent interest rates on their mortgage loans.

A prime loan is for someone with good credit that usually meets all guidelines. In the past, prime loans were only given to people with credit scores in the high 700s. This has dramatically changed as many programs now allow borrowers with credit scores in the 600s to qualify for prime loans.

A prime loan generally has a very good interest rate and very reasonable closing costs. Being in a position to qualify for a prime loan is the ideal situation as it will save a borrower a ton of money.

On the flip side of things, a subprime loan is for someone whose credit situation doesn't meet all guidelines and is generally just a short-term loan, not intended to be held for the life of the loan.

A subprime loan may go to someone who is recently coming out of a bankruptcy, foreclosure, or someone who has a bad past of not paying credit related bills on time and his credit score may be in the low 600s.

Generally, a subprime loan is meant to be kept for only two or three years as it is meant to be refinanced after the borrower has had time to improve his credit by paying his mortgage and other debts on time.

It is important to note that many of the subprime lenders have gone bankrupt and many others have changed their guidelines to require better credit backgrounds than before the subprime housing crisis. If you have less than stellar credit, I would recommend seeking an F.H.A. loan, which comes with a great interest rate since F.H.A. loans are insured by the Federal Housing Administration.

Mortgages Based on Property Use

Not every mortgage is created equal as we will see throughout this chapter, and not every mortgage presents the same amount of risk to the lender. Before a lender decides to loan money to someone, the main objective of the lender is to find out how much risk the particular borrower presents to the potential lender. A portion of the risk level is determined by the borrower's intentions for the subject property. There are generally three types of property: primary residence, second home, and investment property.

Investment Property

Of the three, an investment property is considered the first to go if all income stopped coming in and, therefore, carries the most risk and has the highest interest rate and closing costs. In 2013, a down payment of at least 20% is typical when financing an investment property.

An investment property also usually has tenants that hardly ever treat the home with the same care that the homeowner would, which adds an extra layer of risk that must be paid for by way of a higher interest rate and higher closing costs.

Although I don't recommend them, as they flirt with dishonesty, there are several ways that people try to get around paying this premium if buying an investment property. The most common thing that people have done over the last decade is list the home as a primary residence with the intention of moving into the home within 30 or 60 days after closing.

After moving into the home, with the exception of F.H.A. loans, some lenders have no minimum amount of time that you have to live there to satisfy the owner occupancy requirement before you retreat to a previously owned home or go off and buy a new one. However, it is important to note that many lenders have a one-year occupancy requirement. To give you a clear, ethical illustration of how this works, I'm going to give you the story of Monica. Before I begin with this scenario, I must warn you how important it is to be completely honest with your lender. Not being truthful with your lender is a very serious matter; therefore, be sure to find out the requirements of the lender that you are doing business with and be totally honest.

Monica, who was the owner of two condos in New Jersey, was a business woman living in New Jersey and working in New York. Monica liked living in New Jersey, but she wanted to invest in a new condo that was being built near her place of employment in Manhattan.

When she went online to get mortgage rates, she discovered that marking the home as an investment property versus a primary residence would cost her an extra several thousand dollars and a 2% higher interest rate. She also noticed that it required a much larger down payment.

As she sat at the computer, she wondered how she could get the primary residence rate while still being honest about the situation. She was curious about how long she would have to stay in the home to fulfill the owner occupancy requirement, so she called the 800 number and spoke to one of the loan representatives.

He informed her that as long as she had the intent to move into the home and make it her primary residence within 30 days, it would be eligible for a primary residence rate and costs. He also informed her that after she moved into the home that there was no minimum on how long she had to remain a primary resident of that home.

She knew that this meant that she could move into the home for a year or less and then move out and back into one of her condos in New Jersey. Then she could turn it into an investment property by renting it out to a tenant while keeping her primary residence rate.

She took heed to this information and purchased the home as her primary residence. Instead of moving all of her things from New Jersey, she packed some of her clothes, bought a small amount of furniture, and submitted a change of address with the local post office. She lived at the home for about a year before renting it out and going back to her condo in New Jersey.

Second Home

A second home presents the second highest amount of risk and, therefore, has costs and interest rates that are higher than that of a primary residence but lower than that of an investment property. A second home is usually far away from a person's primary residence and may even be on a beach, such as a condo overseeing the Atlantic in Miami.

Generally, there is not a big difference in pricing between a primary residence and a second home and, depending on the lender, pricing may be the same. However, in 2013, a down payment of at least 10% is typical with most lenders when financing a second home. Some lenders even require a 20% down payment when financing second homes.

One thing a lender won't tolerate is a borrower purchasing a home 10 miles away from his current home and trying to label it as a second home. The mortgage company is going to automatically assume that this is going to be an investment property because of how close it is. The logic behind it is that a reasonable person would not purchase a second home only a few minutes away from his primary residence since a second home is usually used for vacation or some type of getaway. If you are buying a property that you want listed as a second home, depending on the lender, it must be at least 120 miles away from your primary residence.

Primary Residence

A person's primary residence is considered the place where he intends to sleep and eat on a consistent basis. As mentioned before, a home being purchased as a primary residence has the best rates and costs available to a potential borrower. Down payments on primary residences may be as low as 3% in some cases.

This is because a primary residence is considered to have the least amount of risk since a homeowner living in his own property is likely to oversee and take good care of the property. Also, if a person owned a primary residence, a second home, and an investment property and all income stopped coming in, the likely reaction of a reasonable person is to do all that he can to make payments on his primary residence as that is where he lives and shelters his family.

Criteria for Getting a Mortgage

If a person has done all the leg work to getting his credit situation in order, the mortgage qualifying process is generally full of choices more than limitations. The mortgage qualifying process considers three things in order of importance: credit score, debt-to-income ratio (often referred to as DTI), and assets.

Credit Criterion

As told to me by one of my business professors in college, credit is the most important thing, so guard it with your life. Since the financial crisis, many lenders have changed their guidelines to require much better credit backgrounds than before. However, F.H.A. and VA loans are pretty easy to qualify for and allow financing to borrowers with credit scores in the 500s. It is important, however, to not have any late payments on any credit accounts during the two-year period leading to your home purchase and to not have any open collection accounts.

Debt to Income (DTI) Criterion

The debt-to-income ratio, also known as DTI, is very important when applying for a mortgage. The debt-to-income ratio measures the level of debt of a borrower compared to his level of income. Most lenders, in 2013, require debt-to-income ratios to be below 45%, but some are still underwriting loans for borrowers with debt-to-income ratios as high as 50%.

The DTI ratio of a person is calculated by adding up all of a person's debt as it appears in monthly payments on a person's credit report and dividing it by the gross monthly income of the borrower. To give you a clear example of how this works, I will give you the story of Jasmine.

Jasmine was looking to buy a home and had spent the last two years doing all that she could to get her credit in tip-top shape. She knew that her credit was good but now had to figure out how much money she could afford to borrow for a conventional mortgage.

When she called her loan officer at the local bank, after seeing that she had great credit, he told her that he would need to calculate her DTI to figure out how much of a home she could buy since Congress, in 2010, passed legislation that disfavors unconventional approval methods that were used before the credit crisis that didn't require adequate documentation. Now, all lenders must generally make a good-faith determination, based on documented and verified information, that a borrower has the ability to repay the loan.

Because he's a salesman first and a loan consultant second, he invited her down to the bank so he could go over some things with her and ultimately sell her a loan since she had A-1 credit.

The loan officer told Jasmine that there were two ways to figure out her DTI and he wanted to share both ways with her for her own knowledge, which would then make his job easier since he wouldn't have to answer constant questions regarding the matter.

The first way was to add up all of her minimum monthly payments from debt listed on her credit report. On her credit report, she had a car loan that had a monthly payment of $250, three student loans totaling $200 a month, and a credit card with a $30 minimum payment. This put her total monthly debt at roughly $480 a month.

They assumed that Jasmine's mortgage payment, including taxes and insurance, would be roughly $1,200. This then put her total monthly debt at $1,680. Her gross monthly income from her employment was $3,500 on a $42,000 annual salary. To calculate her DTI, they divided the total monthly debt of $1,680 by her monthly gross income of $3,500 and calculated a debt-to-income ratio of 48% ($1,680/$3,500).

The loan officer told Jasmine that they needed to keep the DTI under 50% to make it through underwriting, so she shouldn't choose a home that has a higher monthly payment than the $1,200 they used to calculate her DTI. She stated that she understood and then asked for him to show her the other way to calculate her DTI.

He told her that the other way didn't exactly calculate her DTI, but what it does is it assumes a certain DTI goal and then tells you the maximum monthly payment or total debt that you can have to stay under that stated goal.

Jasmine was slightly confused, so he pulled out a clean piece of paper and started showing her the exact math formula that he was speaking about. He told her that if she wanted to keep her DTI under 50%, she would take her gross monthly income, which was $3,500, and multiply it by .5.

He told her that the $1,750 represented the total amount of debt that she could have as far as minimum monthly payments in order to keep her DTI under 50%. He then told her that she needed to subtract all current debt as shown on her credit report, which included her car payment of $250, her student loans of $200, and her credit card payment of $30.

After subtracting all of her debt from the $1,750 maximum figure, Jasmine was left with $1,270, which represented what could be spent on her new home's mortgage payment.

So, basically, what she did was take her monthly gross income of $3,500 and multiplied it by the desired debt-to-income ratio (in this case 50% or .5), which came out to $1,750. They then subtracted all of her current debt that was listed on her credit report from the $1,750 number. The amount that was remaining came out to be $1,270, which represented the amount that could be spent on a monthly mortgage payment while keeping her debt-to-income ratio under 50%.

As stated earlier, the debt-to-income ratio of a person is very important when applying for a mortgage loan and, just like your credit situation, must be intact and kept under certain limits to be approved.

Assets Criterion

Generally of all three, the assets section isn't as important since the guidelines are generally easy to meet for someone with a good income and savings history. Also, if a rational person (one who uses logic and valid reasoning) has been preparing to purchase a home, he would normally save up money for a down payment and closing costs.

When being qualified for a mortgage loan, the lender wants to make sure that you have the necessary funds to close, which generally include your down payment, closing costs, and several months of reserves. Reserves refer to money that will be remaining in your bank account or liquid investment accounts after closing.

Many lenders require borrowers to have, remaining after closing, enough liquid assets to cover at least three to six months of mortgage payments. This is considered a security cushion in case the borrower has a glitch in employment or falls upon hard times.

Many lenders also require that the assets for closing, as well as any reserves, be seasoned. This means that they want to see that the money has been in the account or at least building for several months. This is because, if given the opportunity, some people who don't have any reserves would just borrow money from a friend or family member and place it into their bank accounts so that it shows on their bank statements.

Types of Mortgages

When deciding on an actual mortgage product, a borrower has a lot of options to choose from based on what his needs are. Although there are possibly more mortgage products available than I care to know about, I will cover the most popular types with you, which include fixed and adjustable loans.

When deciding on a mortgage product, a person needs to have an idea of how long he plans to keep the property, likely rate of appreciation in the area, and if his income will adjust throughout the length of the loan.

After a person successfully answers all of these questions, he should be able to pick the right mortgage product for himself that addresses his needs at the lowest cost possible.

Fixed Rate Mortgage

A fixed rate mortgage is a mortgage where the interest rate and monthly payments stay the same for the duration of the loan. If a person plans to stay in a home for a long time or isn't sure about how long he will stay in a home, I would always recommend going with a fixed rate mortgage. The most popular fixed rates mortgages on the market are the 30-year fixed, 15-year fixed, 40-year fixed, and the 20-year fixed.

30-Year Fixed Mortgage

With a 30-year fixed mortgage, the amount borrowed is amortized over 30 years. The interest at which the money is financed at stays the same for the entire 30 years. During the 30-year period, the monthly mortgage payment stays the same, therefore, making it a fixed mortgage.

If the borrower makes extra payments toward the principal throughout the life of the loan, the monthly payment would still remain the same, and the only adjustment that would be made is to the number of payments that need to be made. This would of course shorten the life of the loan, all depending on how much extra is paid to the principal.

A 30-year fixed mortgage is generally more expensive than many of the other products, as the interest rate is fixed for 30 years, affording the borrower security from interest rate increases. Another reason for the higher cost is the ability to slowly pay back the loan over a 30-year period at the same low rate.

15-Year Fixed Mortgage

A 15-year fixed mortgage is amortized over 15 years and generally comes with a lower interest rate and lower closing costs than a 30-year fixed since you're paying the money back in half the time.

This mortgage is generally for someone who has enough income to afford the higher payments that would come with paying the mortgage off in half the time of a 30-year mortgage and someone who doesn't want to be tied to a mortgage for 30 years.

Although with a 15-year fixed mortgage you are paying the mortgage off in half the time of a 30-year fixed, the mortgage payment is only a 30 to 40 percent increase, which is less than many would think since you're cutting the length of the mortgage in half.

I actually like the 15-year fixed, especially for someone who can afford the slightly higher payments. I also like the fact of being able to own the property outright in 15 years, versus in 30 years, which can seem like a lifetime to some people.

40-Year Fixed Mortgage

The recent emergence of the 40-year fixed has allowed many families in certain areas of the country to afford homes when they would otherwise not be able. As the name indicates, a 40-year fixed mortgage is amortized over 40 years and generally has higher closing costs and interest rates than a 30 and 15-year fixed since you're borrowing the money for a longer period of time.

The 40-year fixed has a lower payment of maybe 10 to 15 percent less than a 30-year fixed, which does wonders for many families living paycheck-to-paycheck.

Other fixed products are available, such as the 20-year and 10-year fixed, which are priced accordingly using the same logic that is used on pricing the other fixed products.

Adjustable Rate Mortgage

An adjustable rate mortgage is a mortgage which, after a certain period of time, the interest rate adjusts. This adjustment is usually upwards and is usually a large adjustment. The way lenders entice homebuyers to take a loan of this nature, knowing that the fixed product with a fixed interest rate is available, is by offering it with lower initial interest rates and closing costs.

Although this type of loan seems dangerous, it does have its perks and in some cases is the best option for someone buying a home and looking for a quality mortgage. A person who should want an ARM is someone who doesn't expect to be in the home long and plans to sell within a set period of time, say three, five, or seven years.

The interest rate tied to an ARM is usually fixed for a certain period of time and then adjusts, generally in accordance to an index, such as the LIBOR. Although the ARM is amortized over a 30-year period, if you plan on being in a home for a while, say at least 10 or 20 years, I recommend staying away from adjustable rate mortgages as they can increase your payment almost double in some scenarios, all depending on the position of the index when the mortgage is due to adjust.

The popularity of each ARM is hard to determine because it all depends on the specific needs and intentions of the borrower. For example, if I were planning to stay in a home for four to five years, I would consider a five-year ARM because it gives me a fixed interest rate for the entire time period that I plan to keep the home.

A few ARM products, listed in order of length, are the 3/1 ARM, 5/1 ARM, and 7/1 ARM. The first number in the equation represents the number of years it is fixed for, and the 1 at the end of the equation represents how often it can adjust. For example, a 5/1 ARM has a fixed interest rate for the first five years and can adjust every one year after that.

3/1 ARM

A 3/1 ARM is a popular product for someone who expects to be in a home for three years or less. The interest rate on the 3/1 ARM is generally less than all other mortgage products since it only gives the borrower a three-year time frame of security where the interest rate is fixed before it adjusts.

The closing costs of a three-year loan are also generally less than most other mortgage products for the same reason as stated above. Anytime a person thinks he will be in the home for longer than three years, I wouldn't recommend a three-year ARM.

5/1 ARM

The 5/1 ARM is very similar to the 3/1 ARM, as it is fixed for a certain period of time before it adjusts. It usually has a slightly higher interest rate than a 3/1 ARM as well as slightly higher closing costs since it gives two more years of security for the borrower. The more security you want from your mortgage loan, the more you will have to pay for it.

Interest-Only Mortgages

An interest-only mortgage provides a borrower with a lower monthly payment than that of a traditional mortgage that pays both principal and interest. An interest-only mortgage is generally amortized over 30 years, but for a certain period of time only interest payments are required.

For example, a 30-year fixed with a 10-year interest-only option would have a fixed interest rate for the entire 30 years, but only interest payments are due in the first 10 years. For the remaining 20 years of the mortgage, it would then basically turn into a 20-year fixed as the entire principal balance would then be amortized over the remaining 20 years of the loan.

Over the last 15 years or so, this product has become extremely popular in places like California and Florida where property values have risen to unaffordable levels. This is just another example of the mortgage industry's attempt to increase profits and give everyone a chance at homeownership.

Interest-only loans generally have a higher interest rate and higher closing costs than a traditional principal and interest loan as the lender assumes more risk since the borrower isn't paying back any principal for a fixed period of time while the mortgage is in the interest-only stage.

Closing Costs

There are practically fees for closing with every mortgage loan. Even though some lenders will deceive you and tell you that they aren't charging you any closing costs for the loan, they are generally just hidden.

What I mean by hidden is that if they are not charged to you up front at closing, they will generally be charged to you by way of a higher interest rate or with pre-payment penalties. It is important to note that many pre-payment penalties have been banned when connected to subprime loans that have adjustable interest rates.

Closing costs are fees associated with the lender providing you with the loan. Lenders will sometimes break the fee down into countless items, which I think is more confusing than anything, and some will just charge you one up-front fee for the loan.

When companies decide to break these fees down, they generally list them as origination, processing, underwriting, discount points (if any), application fee, and several other junk fees. I don't like this idea as what matters to me is the total fee that the lender is charging me for the loan.

I have no desire (and you shouldn't either) to know exactly what department my money is going to because once it's in the lender's hands it can't be of any benefit to me, therefore, leaving me without a reason to care about how the company is going to be dividing the money.

What matters to me is the total fee that I'm paying for the loan to the lender. This is very similar to how many other regular businesses operate. For example, McDonald's doesn't give a breakdown of how the cost of the Big Mac adds up to $3.49. Even if McDonald's did offer a breakdown, there's no reason to want it as the only thing that should matter is the total cost that you are paying for the sandwich.

On top of the fees that the lender charges for the loan, other closing costs would include what are called third parties, which are the appraisal, title insurance, and closing attorney's fees. These fees usually add up to about $1,500 to $2,500 depending on the size and value of the property.

In some states, there are also government and transfer taxes that must be paid at closing, but similar to the third party fees, these are not charges from the lender and will have to be paid no matter what lender you use.

Because closing costs also include third party fees, when the lender fees are broken into 15 different fees, they can be confused as third parties and vice versa. A good way to measure the total lender fees that you are paying from one lender to the next for a loan is to compare the APRs for the same interest rate.

The APR for a mortgage is described as the total cost of the loan put into an annual percentage rate. What this does is it takes the interest rate and adds in the closing costs to come up with the percentage rate that you are actually paying for the loan over the entire duration of the loan.

This is a good way to compare one lender to another. For example, if both companies are offering a 30-year fixed with an interest rate of 6.25%, but the APR for one of the companies is 6.5% versus 6.78% for the other, this would let you know that the company with the higher APR is the one that is charging you the most in lender fees, which is what's important as your third party closing costs and taxes are going to be the same with any lender that you use even if you are told otherwise.

In an attempt to make you think that they have the lower fees, some lenders will sometimes give low-ball estimates on your third-party closing costs to make your total closing costs look less than they really are. This is very deceitful. The way to overcome falling victim to this is to compare the APR between each mortgage company that you are considering doing business with.

Private Mortgage Insurance

Private mortgage insurance, also known as PMI, is required for borrowers that don't have at least 20% down. The borrower pays for the policy that covers the lender in case the borrower defaults on the loan.

Generally, the borrower gets no benefit from paying private mortgage insurance, as the lender is the only one who benefits from it in case the borrower defaults on the loan and the lender is forced to foreclose and sell the property to try to get its investment back.

Where the lender benefits from the private mortgage insurance is, depending on the policy that it has, if it needs to foreclose on the property and sell it, the difference between what it sells the home for and the remaining balance left on the mortgage is made up by the insurance company that underwrote the private mortgage insurance policy.

There are generally two ways to get the PMI taken off. The lender will automatically drop the PMI from your monthly payment, since it is required to do so by law, on the day that your principal balance is scheduled to reach 78% of the original home value as long as you are current on your payments.

The second way to get PMI taken off of your monthly payment applies if your home appreciates in value so that you now have 20% of equity in the home. If this is the case, you must call the lender and pay to have a licensed appraiser come out and appraise the home. If it finds out that the home has appreciated to a point where it gives you 20% of equity, the lender will promptly remove the PMI from your mortgage payment. It is important to note that F.H.A. borrowers will have to pay PMI for a minimum of five years and until their loan-to-value ratios reach 78%, which is the equivalent to having an equity interest of 22% in the home.

PMI is very undesirable. A way to get above 80% financing without having to pay PMI is to get an 80/10 piggy back loan. With an 80/10 loan, you get two separate loans, one for 80% of the mortgage and another for the remaining 10% of the mortgage.

The second mortgage that is for the smaller amount generally has a much higher interest rate than the first mortgage. It is riskier for a lender to have the second position on the home in case of default as it is normally with a totally different lender than the first mortgage.

Even though the interest rate on the second mortgage is generally a lot higher than that of the first, the monthly payment generally still comes out cheaper than doing the one loan that has PMI.

Refinancing

Refinancing a mortgage means getting a new loan on a home that you already own and have a mortgage on or at some point had a mortgage on if it has been paid off. There are two main reasons for a person to refinance a loan: a rate and term adjustment or to get cash out.

Rate and Term Refinance

There are generally two situations when a person would do a rate and term refinance. The first reason is if he has an adjustable rate mortgage that has adjusted or is about to adjust and the borrower wants to lock in a lower fixed interest rate for the remainder of the loan.

The second reason for someone to do a rate and term refinance is if he locked in an interest rate when rates were relatively high and interest rates have come down to where refinancing is a great option in order to lock in a lower payment.

Cash-Out Refinancing

There's generally only one reason to do a cash-out refinance and that is to get some cash out. The reasons why you may want to get the cash out are plenty and may include doing some home improvements, to bail your husband or wife out of jail, or to pay off credit cards.

Generally, when doing a cash-out refinance, some lenders will allow a borrower to raise the loan amount to between 80 and 95 percent of the value of the home; however, with the nation not being far removed from the recent credit crisis, many lenders are only underwriting much lower loan-to-value refinances.

When doing a refinance, both rate and term and cash-out, it's important to know that you have a three-day rescission period after closing and signing all the paperwork to cancel and back out of the loan. The three-day period includes Saturdays but not Sundays and holidays.

If for any reason after closing on a refinance you feel uncomfortable with the new loan that you've selected, you can back out within three days with no penalty.

Home Equity Line of Credit

It is not always prudent for a homeowner to pursue a cash-out refinance. Sometimes a borrower may need to get access to the equity in his home but has an interest rate that is favorable relative to what is available during his time of need. This would make doing a cash-out refinance less than ideal as the homeowner would have to forfeit his current low interest rate.

In such a circumstance, it would be wise to pursue a HELOC that is similar to a secured credit card. A HELOC is a revolving line of credit. With a HELOC, the home is used as collateral and the borrower may borrow up to a maximum amount, which is then paid back using a variable interest rate.

Last Words

Knowing the basics of any business will allow you to operate within that world and at the least give you what you need to be able to oversee a transaction to know what's going on or to see if someone is getting played or not, which is very important as it may be you who's the one that is getting played.

Mortgage information is very valuable since you will need one to invest in one of the best investments in the world. It is also good to know your mortgage options since picking the right mortgage for your situation might determine if the investment that you make is going to be profitable or not.

Chapter 5

Accounting for Investors

When it comes to investing, there are certain accounting basics which must be known and understood very well in order to prevent your investing efforts from becoming gambling, which is the true title for the action that is done when someone without the proper information attempts to invest.

This chapter isn't going to be about traditional accounting that would include talks about inventory and similar topics. This chapter is more about the accounting information needed to make intelligent investment decisions.

From time to time you hear people talking about how certain companies have great stocks or how they are stocks that you must buy. Then when you ask them how much cash the company has on hand they become dumbfounded. If you then ask what are its quarterly liabilities compared to its cash on hand or quarterly income, they may look at you even crazier. Most amateur investors invest on advice that they've received without performing their own due diligence.

To reduce the chances of buying a bad investment, one must be educated on the particulars of what makes a company healthy from a financial point of view. If you knew that a company had quarterly debt obligations of $2 billion and quarterly income of only $1.2 billion on average over the last few years, one might be a little more skeptical about becoming a shareholder.

This company is obviously losing money on a regular basis. Once that happens, it's not too long before talks of bankruptcy emerge and, after that, you can be sure of a declining stock price.

Before investing, it is important to learn where to find such vital information and how to determine if it's good or bad from an investment point of view. This important information is open to the public for all publicly traded companies and can be found on the Yahoo! Finance page after entering the company's ticker symbol for a stock quote.

In my opinion, the three most important sources of information are the balance sheet, income statement, and cash flow statement. In some situations, after looking at a company's balance sheet or income statement, you may be warned that the company needs some immediate medical attention and that it may be dying slowly.

Balance Sheet

The balance sheet can be described as an X-ray of the financial condition of the company. It is divided into three sections: assets, liabilities, and stockholders' equity. The assets section shows how much cash the company has on hand, value of any investments, value of all accounts receivable (money owed to the company), and value of all other assets.

The liabilities section shows everything that the company owes. This will include all accounts payable, long-term debt, and any other dollar amount that the company owed someone at the time of the X-ray. This section is very important and, combined with the assets section, lets you know if the company has enough money to pay its bills if all revenues stopped coming in, which is unlikely with most large companies.

The stockholders' equity section shows the amount of ownership the shareholders as a whole have in the company, which is the result of the amount of assets subtracted by liabilities. In my opinion, the stockholders' equity portion isn't as important as the first two sections but does include such items as treasury stock and retained earnings.

Carefully looking at a company's balance sheet can stop someone from making a very bad investment decision since knowing how much cash a company has versus the amount of its short-term debt obligations can be the deciding factor of success or failure, especially when investing in a small cap company. Although I am not recommending the company's stock, the next page shows a recent copy of Walmart's balance sheet.

View: **Annual Data** | Quarterly Data		All numbers in thousands	
Period Ending	**Jan 31, 2013**	**Jan 31, 2012**	**Jan 31, 2011**
Assets			
Current Assets			
Cash And Cash Equivalents	7,781,000	6,550,000	7,395,000
Short Term Investments	-	-	-
Net Receivables	6,768,000	5,937,000	5,089,000
Inventory	43,803,000	40,714,000	36,437,000
Other Current Assets	1,588,000	1,774,000	3,091,000
Total Current Assets	**59,940,000**	**54,975,000**	**52,012,000**
Long Term Investments	-	-	-
Property Plant and Equipment	116,681,000	112,324,000	107,878,000
Goodwill	20,497,000	20,651,000	16,763,000
Intangible Assets	-	-	-
Accumulated Amortization	-	-	-
Other Assets	5,987,000	5,456,000	4,129,000
Deferred Long Term Asset Charges	-	-	-
Total Assets	**203,105,000**	**193,406,000**	**180,782,000**
Liabilities			
Current Liabilities			
Accounts Payable	59,099,000	55,952,000	52,534,000
Short/Current Long Term Debt	12,719,000	6,348,000	6,022,000
Other Current Liabilities	-	-	47,000
Total Current Liabilities	**71,818,000**	**62,300,000**	**58,603,000**
Long Term Debt	41,417,000	47,079,000	43,842,000
Other Liabilities	-	-	-
Deferred Long Term Liability Charges	7,613,000	7,862,000	6,682,000
Minority Interest	5,395,000	4,446,000	2,705,000
Negative Goodwill	-	-	-
Total Liabilities	**126,243,000**	**121,687,000**	**111,832,000**
Stockholders' Equity			
Misc Stocks Options Warrants	519,000	404,000	408,000
Redeemable Preferred Stock	-	-	-
Preferred Stock	-	-	-
Common Stock	332,000	342,000	352,000
Retained Earnings	72,978,000	68,691,000	63,967,000
Treasury Stock	-	-	-
Capital Surplus	3,620,000	3,692,000	3,577,000
Other Stockholder Equity	(587,000)	(1,410,000)	646,000
Total Stockholder Equity	**76,343,000**	**71,315,000**	**68,542,000**
Net Tangible Assets	**55,846,000**	**50,664,000**	**51,779,000**

Income Statements

As equally important as the balance sheet is the income statement. The income statement has two very simple, but important, sections: revenues and expenses. The revenue section shows all income that the company received during the period and the cost of that revenue (also known as cost of goods sold). The difference between the two is the gross profit or margin. High margins are good, but a margin that is too high may indicate a product or service that is priced inappropriately.

The expense section, on the other hand, has all expenses that the company incurred during the period, such as R&D (research & development), SGA (selling, general, and administrative), and non-recurring expenses.

The difference between the income section and the expense section is the operating income or loss. Subtracted from or added to operating income are items such as expenses related to interest on debt, corporate tax payments, and income received from sources other than its operational activities.

The larger the profit, generally, the better for stock prices. When push comes to shove, revenue and profit growth are the real reasons a company's stock price either appreciates or declines.

It is important to educate yourself in these areas and become a seasoned investor and not someone who takes advice from a financial advisor without doing any of his own due diligence. The next page shows a copy of a recent Walmart income statement.

View: **Annual Data**	Quarterly Data		All numbers in thousands	
Period Ending	**Jan 31, 2013**	**Jan 31, 2012**	**Jan 31, 2011**
Total Revenue	**469,162,000**	**446,950,000**	**421,849,000**
Cost of Revenue	352,488,000	335,127,000	314,946,000
Gross Profit	**116,674,000**	**111,823,000**	**106,903,000**
Operating Expenses			
Research Development	-	-	-
Selling General and Administrative	88,873,000	85,265,000	81,361,000
Non Recurring	-	-	-
Others	-	-	-
Total Operating Expenses	-	-	-
Operating Income or Loss	**27,801,000**	**26,558,000**	**25,542,000**
Income from Continuing Operations			
Total Other Income/Expenses Net	187,000	162,000	201,000
Earnings Before Interest And Taxes	27,988,000	26,720,000	25,743,000
Interest Expense	2,251,000	2,322,000	2,205,000
Income Before Tax	25,737,000	24,398,000	23,538,000
Income Tax Expense	7,981,000	7,944,000	7,579,000
Minority Interest	(757,000)	(688,000)	(604,000)
Net Income From Continuing Ops	17,756,000	16,454,000	15,959,000
Non-recurring Events			
Discontinued Operations	-	(67,000)	1,034,000
Extraordinary Items	-	-	-
Effect Of Accounting Changes	-	-	-
Other Items	-	-	-
Net Income	**16,999,000**	**15,699,000**	**16,389,000**
Preferred Stock And Other Adjustments	-	-	-
Net Income Applicable To Common Shares	**16,999,000**	**15,699,000**	**16,389,000**

Cash Flow Statement

Another important statement is the cash flow statement, which breaks down the adjustments to a company's cash position by category. It shows the adjustments of cash from operating, investment, and financing activities. Companies that report revenue on an accrued basis often report income on its income statement before it is received; however, the cash flow statement shows exactly how much actual money a company received for the quarter or year. With smaller companies that have limited capital, the cash flow statement may be the most important document to analyze.

Free Cash Flow

When a business spends money to buy or improve equipment or real property, it is considered a capital expenditure. Free cash flow is calculated by subtracting capital expenditures from the operating cash flow, both of which are found on the cash flow statement. Free cash flow is a very important metric when determining the health of a company.

To give readers a clear understanding of free cash flow, I will give you the short story of In the Dark Electronics, which I will refer to as IDE. In 2013, IDE had total cash flow from operating activities, which is reported on the first section of a cash flow statement, of $250,000. Capital expenditures, which are reported in the second section of a cash flow statement, were $40,000, which means IDE had $210,000 in free cash flow for 2013.

It is important to know that it is not always a bad sign when a company has free cash flow that is a lot less than the net income reported on its income statement. A business that is expanding will often have a large capital expenditure expense, which must be subtracted from total cash flow from operating activities. On the flip side, a company with a very high free cash flow compared to its income statement's bottom line may not be investing enough into the business to promote growth or to maintain its status as a going concern in a growing and competitive industry.

View: **Annual Data** | Quarterly Data		All numbers in thousands	
Period Ending	**Jan 31, 2013**	**Jan 31, 2012**	**Jan 31, 2011**
Net Income	**16,999,000**	**15,699,000**	**16,389,000**
Operating Activities, Cash Flows Provided By or Used In			
Depreciation	8,501,000	8,130,000	7,641,000
Adjustments To Net Income	394,000	1,515,000	704,000
Changes In Accounts Receivables	(614,000)	(796,000)	(733,000)
Changes In Liabilities	2,313,000	2,746,000	2,243,000
Changes In Inventories	(2,759,000)	(3,727,000)	(3,205,000)
Changes In Other Operating Activities	-	-	-
Total Cash Flow From Operating Activities	**25,591,000**	**24,255,000**	**23,643,000**
Investing Activities, Cash Flows Provided By or Used In			
Capital Expenditures	(12,898,000)	(13,510,000)	(12,699,000)
Investments	(316,000)	(3,548,000)	(202,000)
Other Cash flows from Investing Activities	603,000	449,000	708,000
Total Cash Flows From Investing Activities	**(12,611,000)**	**(16,609,000)**	**(12,193,000)**
Financing Activities, Cash Flows Provided By or Used In			
Dividends Paid	(5,361,000)	(5,048,000)	(4,437,000)
Sale Purchase of Stock	(7,600,000)	(6,298,000)	(14,776,000)
Net Borrowings	1,487,000	3,485,000	7,819,000
Other Cash Flows from Financing Activities	(498,000)	(597,000)	(634,000)
Total Cash Flows From Financing Activities	**(11,972,000)**	**(8,458,000)**	**(12,028,000)**
Effect Of Exchange Rate Changes	223,000	(33,000)	66,000
Change In Cash and Cash Equivalents	**1,231,000**	**(845,000)**	**(512,000)**

Types of Income

It's important to know that there are three different types of income and that they get treated differently for tax purposes. It sounds crazy, but the income which requires sweat and blood is taxed heavier than income that is received without lifting a finger. It sounds backwards. However, instead of fighting it, I recommend adjusting your game plan so the laws become in your favor. The three different types of income are earned income, passive income, and portfolio income.

Earned Income

Earned income is the most commonly received income. When working on a job, the income that is received is considered earned income as it was worked for and, therefore, earned. Earned income is taxed at the highest rates.

Passive Income

Passive income is income that is received without any or much work being done by the investor. Income from having an ownership interest in a limited partnership would be considered passive income, as well as income received from many real estate investments. Passive income is taxed the same way as earned income, except that most real estate income will be tax-free due to the multiple tax deductions involved in having investment real estate.

I would much rather prefer to have passive income versus earned income as it symbolizes that I am receiving income without lifting a finger. As with earned income, people can only get it from one place at a time since they can only be in one place at a time. With passive income, because it generally doesn't require the investor's presence, it can be received from multiple places at once.

Portfolio Income

Portfolio income is income that is received from having ownership in paper assets, such as stocks, bonds, and mutual funds. Dividends from stocks and interest from bonds are examples of portfolio income. Portfolio income is generally taxed at much lower rates than earned and passive income; therefore, portfolio income is very attractive.

Capital Gains & Losses

Stocks and bonds are considered capital assets. If a capital asset is sold for more than it was paid for, it is recognized as a capital gain. On the other hand, if a capital asset is sold for less than it was paid for, then it is considered a capital loss. If the capital asset is held for a minimum of one year before it is sold at a profit, then it would be considered a long-term gain.

The good thing about long-term capital gains is that they are taxed at a maximum rate of 23.8%. Dividends paid on stocks held for more than 60 days are taxed at a maximum of 20%.

Last Words

The accounting basics that were discussed in this chapter are only a small fraction of accounting concepts. However, they are the important basics needed to invest wisely in your mission to becoming financially free.

From reading and carefully analyzing a company's income statement to making investment decisions with the tax rate of different forms of income in mind, this chapter is very important and needs to be understood very well if someone is going to consider becoming an active investor.

Chapter 6

Investing in Stocks

Although stocks may have looked bad in the comparison to real estate, stocks are actually a very good investment if used with a good game plan. I do not, however, believe that a person should limit his investment portfolio to stock investments if the investor has the credit capacity to invest in quality real estate.

What Are They?

Stocks, also known as equities, represent an ownership interest in a corporation, so if you are a shareholder of a particular company, say Home Depot or Nike, you are an owner of that company. Stocks can be divided between common stock and preferred stock. Most of the time when investing in equities, it will be in common stock. Not all companies issue preferred stock, although it does provide a shareholder with certain distinct benefits.

Owners of preferred stock get paid dividends before those of common stock. Also, if the company goes bankrupt, preferred shareholders would get money before owners of common stock. On the downside, only owners of common stock are eligible to vote on issues that require shareholder approval.

Generally, only small amounts of preferred stock get issued as common stock is what's most common as it gives you real ownership powers such as voting on mergers or who should be on the board of directors.

When a business decides to incorporate its operation into a corporation, the company gets authorized to issue a certain number of shares. Incorporating a business and issuing (selling) shares is just like dividing the ownership of a business into many pieces, and whoever holds the most pieces, individually or collectively, has the most control over the company.

Just like any other business, the shareholders of many major companies get their fair share of profits when they are distributed by way of dividends. Shareholders are responsible for voting for the board of directors, who oversee the company and are responsible for hiring the staff for the company's top positions, such as its president and chief executive officer.

Shareholders have the right to attend annual shareholder meetings where they can participate in voting on company issues, such as if the company should merge and become partners with another entity. This means that if you are able to get a large enough share of a company, you can heavily influence the direction of the company and maybe even give yourself a seat on the board.

Most large companies that we buy our everyday products from, such as Walmart, Home Depot, and Target, are considered public companies and have shares that are available for purchase by the general public.

This gives any and everybody, from the President of the United States to the janitor in charge of changing light bulbs at the local hospital, a chance to own a piece of the largest companies in the world. Each company has its own ticker symbol that's used when buying and selling stocks on the stock market. For example, Walmart's ticker symbol is "wmt," and Google's ticker symbol is "goog."

The Best & Worst Times to Invest in Stocks

Besides the abundance of opportunity with investing in real estate, another reason why stocks are not my favorite investment is because many of them do not make wise investments through every part of the business cycle. Certain phases of the business cycle are much better than others for stock investing, and some are just horrible for investing in stocks.

Good Times to Invest in Stocks

The two scenarios that I find to be perfect for investing in stocks are at the trough (lowest point in the business cycle) and during certain parts of an economic expansion. The first scenario is during the lowest point in the business cycle, and that is because when you are at the bottom, the only way you can go is up. Generally, at this point in the cycle, all of the amateur investors have sold off all of their good investments for relatively low prices to astute investors who understand when to be greedy.

The second scenario is when the economy is going through a lengthy expansion with very low interest rates as well as little to no inflation. This is a perfect scenario as it usually indicates that the economy is flourishing and stocks will generally be the benefit. Usually, in most expansions, the demand for goods is so high that inflation gets out of control, which leads to rising interest rates.

So, if an expansion is present with both low inflation and low interest rates, it is usually a great time to invest in stocks as corporate profits will likely continue to increase and set new earnings records, which normally will increase a company's stock price.

A Bad Time to Invest in Stocks

When the economy is expanding and signs start arising that the peak is near and that a retraction is coming, it is usually a very bad time to invest in stocks. Generally, during an expansion that is nearing its peak, the Federal Reserve will usually raise interest rates in order to counter inflation that eventually accompanies an expansion and economic activity will begin to decline. Usually, the new and continuing unemployment claims will start to increase and many economic reports, including housing starts and the retail sales report, will start reporting stagnate or declining growth when the peak is near.

Don't Even Think About It

The worst time to invest in a stock is when you receive an email or fax telling you that a company is getting ready to explode. This is often considered a hot stock tip, which is a scam 99% of the time. Generally, when you receive one of these faxes or emails, it is from someone who is looking to inflate the stock price and then quickly sell his shares before the stock price drops back down to its true value, which is often $0.

Also, it is important to be careful whom you accept investment advice from as people who receive the hot stock tip will often attempt to pass it on to you without telling you where they got the information from. When it comes to buying stocks based on this information, do your family and yourself a big favor and don't even think about it.

Exchange Markets

There are many exchange markets, but only two exist that I feel the need to cover. The exchange markets which I'm going to cover in order of popularity are the New York Stock Exchange (NYSE) and NASDAQ.

New York Stock Exchange

The New York Stock Exchange (NYSE) was created in 1792 and is the largest exchange for stocks in the world. It is commonly referred to as the "Big Board" and it is the home to many of the largest companies in the world.

Elite companies such as Walmart, Exxon Mobil, Home Depot, and Target have all decided to have their shares traded on the New York Stock Exchange. It is very likely that when investing in stocks, the company that you have bought a piece of ownership in will be listed on the New York Stock Exchange.

The New York Stock Exchange has thousands of listed companies, and they all pay a pretty penny to have their companies listed and traded. In addition to that nice ransom, all listed companies have to meet strict requirements relating to the value of the stock, number of shareholders, and company earnings.

The majority of all companies listed on the NYSE are going concerns, and the ones who lose their stability generally get delisted or kicked off of the exchange. Stocks begin trading on the NYSE at 9:30 a.m. Eastern time and close at 4:00 p.m. The NYSE is open Monday through Friday and is closed for most recognized holidays.

NASDAQ

Behind the NYSE, I consider NASDAQ as the most prestigious exchange in North America and possibly in the world. Although it may have sounded like every big company is a member of the NYSE, there are many very high profile companies that are listed on the NASDAQ.

The NASDAQ is often regarded as the exchange for tech stocks and is home to big names, such as Microsoft, Intel, Cisco, and Apple Computers. Similar to the NYSE, there are very strict guidelines that must be met in order to be listed on the NASDAQ; therefore, most companies listed on the NASDAQ are quality companies in terms of having a certain level of income and assets.

During the tech boom in the late 90s and early 2000s, many companies that were traded on the NASDAQ became extremely overpriced and were the reason behind the infamous bubble burst. A lot of these companies had stock prices that were rapidly appreciating, but the companies weren't making any profits. This definitely caught up to investors as the true value eventually came to light on many of these companies and, in some instances, the true value that was discovered was $0.

Types of Orders

Before making any investment decisions involving stocks, it is essential to know what type of orders can be made and how to read certain pertinent information that will be displayed to you when researching various companies' stock information.

First and foremost, it is important to know and understand some basic, yet important, terminology. When receiving a stock quote, there are generally three important things that you should want to know right away. The first is the current market price of the stock. This is established as the last price that the stock was sold for. When you hear that a stock is trading at $25 per share, this means that the last trade of the stock between a buyer and a seller was for $25.

The next two important things that you should know and understand are the bid and ask price. The bid price represents the highest price that someone is willing to pay for the stock at any given moment, and the ask price represents the lowest price that a seller is willing to sell the stock for.

Something very important for you to know is that anytime the bid price is higher than the current or last price, someone is willing to pay more than the stock's current market price, which will raise the price of the stock to the latest purchase price if the person bidding is successful at buying shares.

Also, if the bid price is far below the last price, that means that the market is not in high demand of that particular company's stock at its current price, and if the stock is sold below current market value, the stock price will decrease as the value or stock price only represents the last price that the stock was sold for.

On the flip side, if both the bid price and the ask price are far above the current market price and the two meet somewhere above current market value, the stock price will increase accordingly.

When placing orders to purchase stocks, there are several options that a person can choose from when deciding what type of order to make, and I'll be discussing the ones that I feel are important for you to know.

Market Order

A market order is the most common type of order in the market place. A market order doesn't request that the stocks be bought or sold at a certain price. It just asks that the transaction takes place at whatever the going rate is in the market place.

When someone makes a market order request, he is not concerned with buying or selling at a certain price and is generally comfortable with whatever the going rate is at the time of the request. For example, if someone makes a market request to buy shares of Home Depot and the going price is $29, then that is the price that he is usually going to pay.

Buy Limit Order

A buy limit order is an order that requests that the designated stock be purchased at a certain price or below. For example, if Walmart's stock is trading at $49, and an investor wants some but doesn't think it is worth more than $47, he or she can put in a buy limit order of $47. When the stock price dips down to $47 or below, the stock will be purchased for the going price as long as it is less than $47.

A buy limit order is a very good way to prevent an investor from paying more than a certain price for a stock, especially if you've noticed a high level of volatility in the price of the stock and want to capitalize and buy it.

For example, if you noticed that Exxon Mobil's stock price constantly fluctuated from $65 to $67 on a daily basis and you wanted to buy some at the low point, then a buy limit order at $65 would buy the stock for you when it was again available at $65.

Sell Limit Order

A sell limit order is very similar to a buy limit order but, as the name indicates, it involves selling a stock instead of buying one. A sell limit order is a request to sell a stock at or above a certain price. This sell limit price is usually higher than the current market price.

For example, let's use help from the fictitious example above and say that after buying the Exxon Mobil stock for $65 that you wanted to sell it as soon as the price went back up to $67. In this case, you would place a sell limit order of $67, and as soon as the going rate was $67 again, your stock would be sold, therefore, making you a quick profit.

A sell limit order is a good way to sell a stock at a certain price without having to watch the market until it is paying a certain amount for the stock. With a sell limit order, you can just place it, and whenever the stock price goes back up, your shares would automatically sell if there are buyers in the market.

Sell Stop Order

A sell stop order is a good way to protect against losses when stock trading. A sell stop order is always placed below the current market price and triggers as soon as the stock reaches or goes below the sell stop order price. For example, if an investor owned shares of Apple and placed a sell stop order for $300, it would trigger and turn into a market order as soon as the stock fell to $300 or below. This would prevent the investor from taking any further losses.

Buy Stop Order

When short-selling, a buy stop order can be a good friend to an investor. A buy stop order is always placed above the current market price. It triggers and becomes a market order as soon as the stock reaches the designated price. For example, if an investor were to short shares of Google for $850, he could place a buy stop order to purchase the stock as soon as the price reaches or surpasses $875 or any other arbitrary number. It is important to note that I do not recommend shorting Google under any circumstance other than in the unlikely event of evidence surfacing that it has cooked all of its financial records for the last ten years.

Classification of Stocks

Stocks are often classified based on the type of company that it is, the company's value, or, in some cases, the level of growth that is expected from the company. Before investing in a particular company, it is very important to get to know the company on a personal level and find out what the company's goals and objectives are for the short and long term. Some companies are growth minded, while some are defensive minded and operate in services that are always in high demand.

In order to prosper in the world of stock investing, a person must have a clear understanding of what he is doing or he shouldn't be doing it at all. Investing in stocks can be very risky, depending on the level of knowledge held by the person making the investment decisions. Below is a list of classifications that are important to know.

Blue Chip Stocks

Blue chip stocks represent the largest companies in the world, such as Walmart, American Express, and Home Depot. These companies usually have very high earnings year after year and have a reputation of stability and exceptional corporate management. These companies have great financial strength and often share the profits of the business on a quarterly basis with their shareholders.

Growth Stocks

Growth stocks, which often trade at relatively high valuations, are companies that have the opportunity to grow both sales and profits at faster rates than their industries and the market as a whole. These companies are usually very aggressive and have plans for expansion that will likely create shareholder value if properly executed.

Many growth stocks don't pay dividends to their shareholders as many of the companies retain the profits to grow the company, which can often mean acquiring other companies. If you are looking for a safe company that will pay you dividends every quarter, a growth stock is probably not what you are looking for.

Value Stocks

Value stocks, which are considered undervalued by the market, trade at lower valuations than their growth counterparts and many value stocks pay dividends to their shareholders, which, if reinvested, can make the right value stock a much better investment than most growth stocks. Value stocks often are companies that are not growing at exceptional levels but often have great balance sheets and substantial market share.

Income Stocks

Income stocks are generally some of my favorite stocks as they offer above average dividend payments to their shareholders. These companies are usually very stable and can afford to reward their shareholders. I believe that a quality company that pays a consistent dividend is worthy of being owned throughout the business cycle. A downside to owning many income stocks, however, is that they can be sensitive to interest rate hikes and can often decline in value when there is speculation that the FOMC will take action to increase interest rates.

Defensive Stocks

Defensive stocks are companies that are generally stable in all economic climates since they provide important goods and services that are used in both good and bad economic times. These would include shares of utility companies, food suppliers, tobacco companies, and beverage companies.

Defensive stocks usually pay dividends and the best of the companies in this category often survive during the worst of economic times, which is why defensive stocks are relatively good investments during the tougher parts of the business cycle. On the downside, however, defensive stocks don't have as much potential for growth during economic expansions, which means that returns will be limited.

Large Cap Stocks

Large cap stocks include many of the blue chip companies that are powerhouse businesses and have a large piece of the market share. This is not always the case as some large cap companies have negative earnings and declining sales.

This is possible because, unlike blue chip companies that get their title from being stable, proven companies that have track records of exceptional execution and profit growth, a large cap company is just a company with a market capitalization of over $10 billion. The market capitalization of a company is determined by multiplying the company's stock price by the number of shares outstanding.

During the period right before the tech stock bubble burst is a good example of when many companies that didn't make any profits, but because of inflated stock prices, were labeled as large cap companies.

Mid Cap Stocks

A mid cap company is a company with a market capitalization of greater than $2 billion but less than $10 billion. Generally, a mid cap company will not pay any dividends if it is attempting to execute a growth strategy since it will usually use all of the company's profits to expand.

Small Cap Stocks

Small cap stocks are stocks of companies that have less than $2 billion in market capitalization. Many small cap companies don't pay any dividends as they generally need every dollar that they can get to help either expand the business or, in many scenarios, to remain a going concern. Many small cap companies are acquired by larger companies and are often bought for trade, by some speculative traders, as potential acquisition targets.

Private Equities

A lot of money can be made investing in private equities. Private equities are companies that are not listed on any public exchange and often are not registered with the Securities & Exchange Commission. These companies are usually pretty small and, therefore, offer a lot of upside and are, for the most part, only available to accredited investors since they are considered very risky. Although private equities are not listed on any public exchanges, there are private exchanges, such as NYPPEX and Private Equity Exchange, which allow accredited investors to trade private securities.

Accredited investors include individuals with a net worth, excluding primary residence, exceeding $1 million. Annual income of $200,000 for an individual or joint income of $300,000 for a married couple also qualifies as accredited. Investment firms and banks are other examples of accredited investors.

Private equities are often confused with private equity firms. Private equity firms are usually limited partnerships that raise capital from institutional investors, such as hedge funds and pension funds, and acquire controlling interests of companies that are believed to be undervalued by the firm.

Business Development Companies

Business development companies invest in small businesses and offer relatively high dividend payments since they are required to distribute at least 90% of taxable income to shareholders. In addition to relatively high dividend payments, another benefit of business development companies is that they generally pay no or very little corporate income tax, which allows more capital to be passed down to shareholders.

Mutual Funds & Exchange-Traded Funds

With all the talk of the need for diversification in today's marketplace, a lot of people are turning to mutual funds. A mutual fund invests in a collection of companies from different sectors, industries, market caps, and often countries.

If a person buys one share of a mutual fund, he could possibly own a piece of approximately 100 companies. To some people this is considered diversification as they own a piece of many companies instead of just one or a few.

For the record, I believe diversification is being in several totally different investments. For example, owning two hotels, a book publishing company, a fashion brand, and shares of Coca-Cola and Exxon Mobil would symbolize diversification to me. It doesn't have to be in these specific businesses or stocks, but hopefully you get the picture.

In regards to having a diversified portfolio, my opinion on mutual funds is that they are for amateur investors who don't know how to pick their own investments or for experienced investors who, for one reason or another, don't have the time to research and stay familiar with quality investments.

Although mutual funds can give a person professional management of investments, the downside to that is that mutual funds generally charge large fees that eat a large portion of the profits on a continual basis. I'm not at all a fan of this, especially when the mutual fund company doesn't assume any of the risk.

On the upside, there are mutual funds which are tied to indexes, such as the S&P 500, that have much smaller fees than traditional mutual funds since less work and research are performed since they are just tied to a particular index.

Exchange-traded funds offer a similar level of diversification and can be used to invest in specific sectors, including a plethora of funds that allow you to benefit greatly when the market experiences a downturn. Although I don't recommend leveraged funds for most investors, there are many ETFs that provide a person with greater exposure to the market and allow an investor to double or triple returns. However, it should be noted that when using leveraged funds, possible losses have the ability to double and triple as well, which is why I don't recommend them to general audiences.

There are two benefits of using ETFs as an investment vehicle, in my opinion, that makes them favorable to mutual funds. First, the shares of an ETF can be traded like a stock, which means that they can be purchased and sold during the day when the market is open. Mutual funds, on the other hand, only allow for selling at the end of a trading day, which can expose an investor to great losses in the event of unexpected market volatility. Also, total management fees are often less with ETFs than with a mutual fund, which can make a substantial difference when calculating an investment's long-term return.

Depending on the investment skill level of the individual, mutual funds or ETFs may need to play a vital role in a person's investment portfolio in order to give him some level of diversification that he would normally not otherwise have if making all investment decisions on his own.

Hedge Funds

Hedge funds, which are lightly regulated, are very popular investment vehicles that are limited to wealthy and sophisticated investors. The first known hedge fund was created in 1949 by Alfred Jones, who believed in having long positions on assets that he expected to outperform the general market and selling short assets that he expected to underperform the general market. Such a strategy was seen as a hedge to the risks inherent in the market; therefore, the term hedge fund was created.

Although not always, the typical hedge fund is formed as a limited liability partnership. The investors are the limited partners and the general partner is usually the investment manager, which is often a separate company that has been hired by the hedge fund. Some of the best hedge fund managers have been known to outperform the general market during both ascending and descending markets. Although the best hedge fund managers seek exceptional returns for their investors, they also take pride in respecting their duty of managing risk, which is just as important as managing returns and may result in a fund underperforming the market.

Hedge funds usually have a 2/20 fee structure that pays the investment manager an annual 2% management fee, which is based on the net asset value of the fund. The fund manager also receives 20% of the annual profit, which is referred to as carried interest.

All of the fund's expenses are usually taken from the 2% management fee.

Hedge funds employ a variety of strategies with the most common funds having both long and short positions in equities. Many hedge funds are highly leveraged, which allows them to invest with assets that far outweigh the assets that actually belong to their funds. This can dramatically increase the return that a fund can achieve, while also increasing the level of risk. However, many fund managers will apply the least amount of leverage to the riskiest assets and the most amount of leverage to investments with the least amount of risk. The following are a few things about hedge funds that should be understood before investing as a limited partner of a hedge fund.

Hurdle Rates

A hurdle rate is not used in all hedge funds; however, funds with hurdle rates require the fund to achieve a certain return before the fund pays the investment manager a performance fee. Hurdle rates are usually small and may range from 4 to 6 percent and no performance fee may be paid until the fund reaches the set return. For example, a fund with a hurdle rate of 5% will not pay a performance fee to the fund's manager until the fund surpasses a 5% return.

High Water Marks

High water marks prevent investment managers from being paid on the same returns twice. When a fund has a decrease in net asset value, the fund manager will not be paid a performance fee until the net asset value surpasses the previous peak in net asset value which was used to pay a prior performance fee. For example, if a fund paid a performance fee when the fund had a net asset value of $10 million, and then the fund's net asset value decreases to $9 million, the fund would not be obligated to pay a performance fee until the fund's net asset value surpasses the $10 million mark. The return from $9 million in net asset value to $10 million would not be considered a basis for a performance fee because of the high water mark provision. I recommend not investing in any hedge fund that doesn't have a high water mark provision.

Surrender fees

Surrender fees, which are also commonly known as redemption or withdrawal fees, charge investors a set percentage for withdrawing money from the fund. The terms for surrender fees may vary; however, most funds will typically only charge surrender fees for withdrawals that occur within a certain period of time or for withdrawals that occur outside of acceptable withdrawal periods. In many cases, the surrender fee is returned to the fund and benefits the remaining investors. Sometimes, however, the surrender fee is retained by the investment manager for his benefit.

Short-Selling

Short-selling is a great way to profit from equities in a falling market. Short-selling involves an investor borrowing securities from a broker and selling them. This transaction is based on the assumption that the underlying security will decrease in value, which will allow the investor to repurchase the shares at a later date (at a lower price) and return them to the broker. Without regard to fees that must be paid to the broker for borrowing such shares, the difference between what the shares are initially sold for and what they are repurchased for is the profit (or loss) for the investor.

Short-selling can be very dangerous in a rising market. Even in a declining market, there is a substantial amount of risk involved when short-selling. After going short on an equity, if it rises in value, the investor would be required to repurchase the shares at a much higher cost than what he was able to sell them for initially. Without owning an equal amount of the shares that are sold short, one way to limit the risk that is inherent with short-selling is to buy call option contracts on the same stock; therefore, if the stock has an unexpected increase in price, the investor would be covered since he has the option to purchase the stock at a price that is either the same, slightly lower, or slightly higher than the price that the shares were at when they were initially sold by the investor.

Margin Trading

Margin trading is a good way to increase your rate of return if you are an astute investor; however, margin trading also has substantial risks that can quickly deplete an account if the wrong investments are purchased on margin. Margin trading involves borrowing money, with interest being charged, from your brokerage firm to purchase stocks, which become collateral that the brokerage firm can sell to cover a margin call. FINRA (Financial Industry Regulatory Authority) requires that investors with margin accounts maintain a minimum of 25% in equity of the total market value of all securities in the margin account. Some firms, however, have larger maintenance requirements than the legally required 25%. If an investor's equity goes below the required maintenance level, a margin call will generally be placed for the investor to deposit more money or to sell shares to bring the account into compliance.

By law, a brokerage firm is required to obtain an investor's signature before allowing him to trade on margin. Also, by law, an investor is required to deposit at least $2,000 with his brokerage firm before being allowed to trade on margin. Although some brokerage firms allow less to be borrowed, Regulation T of the Federal Reserve Board allows an investor to borrow up to 50% of the price of securities. This is referred to as the initial margin requirement. The 25% rule that I mentioned, however, refers to the maintenance margin requirement and only applies after securities are purchased.

Fundamental Analysis

When investing in stocks, choosing wisely can be just as important as it is with purchasing real estate. Knowing when a stock is underpriced or overpriced can be a very powerful skill that can make or save an investor a ton of money.

There are certain tools that will be explained in this section that can be used in what is considered fundamental analysis. Fundamental analysis does not focus on trading patterns as much as it does the financial condition of a company and its stock price in relation to its earnings.

The following ratios are used in fundamental analysis to examine the condition of a company and its stock price to help an investor make a wise investment decision.

Earnings per Share (EPS)

The earnings per share figure of a company is closely watched by Wall Street and is used to determine if a company met its earnings goal and Wall Street expectations. A company's earnings per share is calculated by subtracting money paid out for preferred dividends from the net income and then dividing the remaining figure by the number of shares outstanding (owned by the public).

For the sake of doing easy math, let's say that Nike had an annual profit of $10,500 and paid out $500 in preferred dividends. That would then leave $10,000 to be divided by the number of shares that are outstanding. Let's say that Nike only had 1,000 shares outstanding. That would then give it an earnings per share of $10 ($10,000/1,000 =$10).

Often, when a company's earnings are released on a quarterly basis, the EPS figure is usually what matters most to both individual and institutional investors. Generally, if a company misses its goal or comes short of Wall Street's (research analysts that cover the stock) expectations for earnings or revenue, the stock price will immediately fall. On the other hand, if a company's earnings come back stronger than expected, the stock price will generally increase.

When earnings are equal to goals and expectations, the stock price usually isn't disturbed much since stocks constantly adjust based on expected future earnings. It is very important to know that a stock may have a large increase or decrease in price if the company, when releasing earnings, offers a future forecast of earnings, revenue, or margin that is different from expectations.

Price-to-Earnings Ratio

The price-to-earnings ratio of a company is also very heavily watched by Wall Street. A company's price to earnings (P/E) ratio is often used to measure if a company is trading for more than it is worth based on its earnings.

A company's price-to-earnings ratio is calculated by dividing its current market price by its earnings per share. For example, let's say that Nike was currently trading at $30 and had an earnings per share figure of $10 (based on example above for EPS). To find the company's price-to-earnings ratio, you would divide the $30 share price by the $10 earnings per share figure ($30/$10 = 3).

This would be a very attractive P/E if true. Depending on the industry and the potential for future growth that a company may have, a good investment usually has a low P/E of no more than 20. Otherwise, it may take a very long time before you see a satisfying return.

In some cases, a company's stock price might be low due to talks of bankruptcy or a possible government investigation into some of the company's practices. So just because a company has a high earnings per share figure and a low price-to-earnings ratio, it doesn't mean that you should automatically invest in that company.

PEG Ratio

The PEG ratio is very important and is preferred by many investors and analysts over the P/E ratio to determine if a company is fairly priced. The PEG ratio divides a company's price-to-earnings ratio by its expected annual EPS growth. The expected growth rate used to calculate a company's PEG ratio is often based on three or five years of projections. A PEG ratio of 1 or less is ideal. For example, if a company has a P/E ratio of 20 and has expected EPS growth of 20%, the PEG ratio would be 1. Generally, the only time I would recommend or consider buying a stock with a P/E ratio of more than 20 is if the expected growth rate meets or exceeds the P/E ratio. However, a company can just be in growth mode and may have exceptional sales growth that doesn't immediately make its way to the company's bottom line. In this type of scenario, I may invest in a company if the expected sales growth and business model lead me to believe that the increase in sales will eventually lead to increased profits.

Return on Equity

A company's return on equity is determined by dividing the company's net income by the shareholders' equity. This ratio is very important and measures how well a company has used its shareholders' equity to fund new earnings growth. The higher the return on equity, the better the potential is for share price growth. Unless there is a reason to believe that a company has great growth potential, a 10% or higher yearly return on equity over a three-year period is required to get my attention.

Debt to Equity

The debt-to-equity ratio is used to determine how leveraged a company is financially. It compares a company's debt to its equity. Companies are usually financed by issuance of stocks and bonds. The more bonds that are issued by the company, the higher its long-term debt will be. Although sometimes all debt is included, this ratio usually only considers long-term debt and divides it by the shareholders' equity, both of which are found on a company's balance sheet.

This ratio is imperative when considering the long-term viability of a company. When a company goes bankrupt, it is usually because of maturing debt that is unable to be satisfied or restructured. In some cases, the interest payments alone are so expensive that a company can't pay them and defaults on its debt, resulting in the need for bankruptcy protection. Also, when a company has heavy debt commitments, it is usually very hard for the company to grow since so much revenue is used to offset debt, and there often times isn't sufficient remaining capital for marketing, research & development, and asset acquisitions, all of which lead to growth.

Depending on the industry, a debt-to-equity ratio less than 0.33 is usually great, and a ratio of less than 0.5 is still very solid.

Current Ratio

The current ratio of a company measures its ability to pay its short-term obligations over the next 12 months from current assets, such as cash and cash equivalents. The current ratio is determined by dividing current assets as stated on the balance sheet by the company's current liabilities, which are also on the balance sheet.

A current ratio above two is considered satisfactory. However, what is considered satisfactory often varies depending on the company and industry. If a company has a current ratio of two, this would indicate that the company has twice as many current assets as current liabilities. If a company has a current ratio of less than one, this would indicate that the company may have trouble satisfying short-term obligations, all depending on how fast the company can turn over its inventory or raise capital.

Depending on the industry, a current ratio that is too high may indicate that a company has too many current assets and may need to do a better job of investing extra cash into higher earning assets.

Technical Analysis

Although not as important as fundamental analysis when long-term investing, technical analysis, which includes a lot of chart studying, provides a far better set of tools for short-term trading. Many times investors will attempt to make short-term trades in great companies after performing the due diligence that is required for making long-term investments. This approach, although having its benefits, is generally a recipe for unexpected short-term results.

A great company that has an unbelievable valuation can trade sideways, meaning within a limited range, for a long period of time before it is properly appreciated by the market. Someone looking for short-term gains may not be able to achieve them if he only performs a fundamental analysis on the company, which is why searching for stocks that have strong technicals, such as an uptrend line, a reasonable level of support, and trading above moving-day averages, is very important.

Support & Resistance

When analyzing a stock chart, it is important to know if the equity is being supported or restrained by a floor or a ceiling. A support level can be described as a price range where the stock seems to have buyers willing to purchase in the event of a price decline. If you notice that over a certain period that the price of a stock fluctuates but never drops below a certain level, this may indeed be a level of support. It is important to know that if a stock drops substantially below any perceived levels of support, it is considered a breakthrough and may continue to drop until it finds its next level of support.

A level of resistance describes a perceived ceiling for the price of an equity. If you notice that during a certain period that a company's stock price fluctuates but never surpasses a certain level, this may be a level of resistance, which is usually an indication that the stock will need a catalyst to elevate it and allow it to break through the perceived ceiling.

Being able to determine if a particular stock has a level of support or resistance can help a trader profit greatly from price movements and also helps when speculating on an investment's potential risk versus its potential reward.

Trends

It is very important to be able to identify both uptrend lines and downtrend lines. The movement of stock prices has a propensity to fall into trends and knowing the direction of the trend can make for some very easy trading profits.

An uptrend line has a positive slope that connects two or more low points, and the second low point must be higher than the first. As long as the stock's price remains above the trend line, the trend is considered intact and, to some degree, can be relied upon. Uptrend lines can often indicate potential areas of support, and I do not advise selling short any company that has an uptrend line.

I also do not recommend ever buying a stock that is trending upwards if it has a poor valuation. Although most traders consider the technicals more than the fundamentals when trading, I think that the fundamentals must also be considered with every company that an investor buys, including for purchases that are made when short-term trading.

A downtrend line, on the other hand, has a negative slope that connects two or more high points, and the second high point must be lower than the first. Downtrend lines can often act as a means for resistance, and I do not advise going long on any equity that is experiencing a downward trend.

Moving Averages

Similar to trend lines, moving averages can aid in determining potential levels of support and resistance. The two that I pay the most attention to are the 50 and the 200-day moving averages. Moving averages are simply the average closing prices of stocks over a select period. Although the efficacy of using moving averages has diminished greatly over the last couple of decades, buying or remaining long in a stock when it is trading above both its 50 and 200-day moving averages is a strategy that is currently used by many on Wall Street.

Advance-Decline Ratio

The advance-decline ratio compares the number of stocks that have increased in price compared to the prior session's close and also compares the number of stocks that have declined compared to the previous session's close. In a bull market, the number of advancers usually is a lot higher than the number of decliners.

One thing to watch out for is a stock market that is increasing in value but one that has consisted of more stocks declining than advancing. This is possible when the gain of select stocks within an index advance substantially enough to have a net-positive impact on the market. It is important to know that I do not consider any broad market uptrend to be credible unless more stocks are routinely advancing than declining.

Dividends

Dividends are the portion of company profits that the board decides to share with the company's shareholders. When declared, dividends are usually paid on a quarterly basis. Not all companies pay dividends as many of them need the profits for growing the business.

One of the most important things to know about dividends is the ex-dividend date. If an investor buys a company's stock on or after the ex-dividend date, he will not be entitled to the dividend payment that has been declared. Also, if you sell a company's stock after a dividend has been declared but before its ex-dividend date, the new owner of the shares will be entitled to receive the dividend payment. I like to use Dividend.com as a quick resource for checking a company's dividend schedule, including its ex-dividend date.

Stock Splits

There are generally two scenarios when a company will decide to do a stock split. The first will be to decrease the price of its stock to make it more attractive to new investors, and the other would be a reverse stock split to increase the price of a stock to make it more attractive.

The first scenario, which is to decrease the stock price to make it more attractive, would happen if the stock price has grown rapidly and the price no longer appears attractive to new investors. The company would usually perform a 2-for-1 stock split. This would give all investors two shares for each one share that they currently own, and it would reduce the stock price in half. This doesn't add any profit or gain to the stock but only makes it more attractive.

For example, let's say that the high demand for oil raised Exxon Mobil's stock price to $150 per share. This price is considered relatively high, and the company would probably decide to do a 2-for-1 stock split. This would reduce the stock price to $75 and double the amount of shares that a particular investor currently has, which doesn't change the total value of the stock owned by the investor.

Let's say Denise owned 10 shares of the stock at $150 per share for a total value of $1,500. After the 2-for-1 stock split, Denise would then own 20 shares of the stock valued at the split price of $75 per share, leaving her total value at $1,500. The stock split only made the stock price more attractive to new investors.

The other scenario that would lead a company to do a stock split is if the stock price is relatively low and unattractive. This would be the case if the stock price is very low and nobody wants to invest in it because the public thinks the low stock price makes it appear that it is a poor performing company, which isn't always the case.

In this case, a company would generally do a reverse stock split. Let's say that a company's stock price decreased to $2 per share. At this point, many investors would think the company is getting close to being delisted from the New York Stock Exchange and possibly headed toward bankruptcy. To help ease investor concerns, the company may decide to do a 1-for-10 stock split.

A 1-for-10 stock split would multiply the stock price by 10, making the value $20 per share instead of $2, and it would reduce or divide the number of shares owned by 10. For example, let's say that Tina owned 100 shares of Ford's stock at $2 per share, for a total value of $200. After the company performed the 1-for-10 reverse stock split, Tina would only own 10 shares of the stock that would be valued at $20 per share, therefore, leaving her total value at $200.

Stock splits are universally common for profitable companies during extended economic expansions when stock prices are generally increasing across the board. During the economic expansion of the 90s, it was common for a growth or blue chip company to perform a stock split every few years to keep the stock price from appearing unattractive.

Day Trading & Short-Term Trading

Because day trading can sometimes be more emotional than rational, I do not recommend it to new investors since new investors usually haven't learned to control their emotions when it comes to investing their money. Learning to control your emotions in relation to your finances usually takes some maturing, losing money, and watching the cycle of stock prices as well as the economy.

Usually, I will only day trade unintentionally as I might buy a company that increases dramatically in value that same day, which will entice me to sell and take my quick profit. However, I am a huge fan of short-term trading. In this practice, I buy or short a stock the day before its earnings are scheduled to be released. In some cases, I will buy or short a stock after its earnings are released if I believe that the stock has momentum in either direction.

Most of the time, however, I will buy either call or put option contracts instead of buying the actual stock itself to limit my exposure to risk and profit if the stock does move in the direction that I believe it will after the company's earnings are released.

It is common and wise to only day trade with stocks that have large average trading volumes since all stocks don't trade large amounts every day, and it is hard to day trade with a stock that doesn't have a daily demand. For the record, most stocks that are traded on the New York Stock Exchange and on NASDAQ have pretty high trading volumes.

It is also very common to day trade stocks that fluctuate very often. For example, if a company's stock price goes from $10 to $12 and back again on a daily basis for 10 straight trading days, many day traders will consider trading this stock in order to take advantage of the large and predictable range of fluctuation.

The biggest reason why I usually don't recommend day trading for new investors is because many times an amateur investor will buy a company with the purpose of day trading that he would not have purchased if he were not intending to day trade. A lot of times when attempting to day trade, people will completely disregard their trading principles when greed takes over. It is important to not make emotional investment decisions, especially when attempting to day trade, and if you're not 100% sure that you have your emotions in check, don't even think about day trading.

Options Trading Basics

Options, which are also referred to as derivatives, can be very risky if used the wrong way. They can also be very rewarding if used correctly, similar to any investment, but it is much more serious with options as you could potentially lose more money than you can dream of.

Options are a very good investment if you are the one buying them and potentially suicide if you are the one selling them. On the positive side, purchasing the right kind of option can be like having insurance on your stock in case the price declines. Also, a certain option can be purchased on a stock that you don't own, and if the stock price rapidly increases, your option gives you the right to buy the stock at the low price that's agreed to on your option.

Let's take a look at some of the option choices out there and which ones to stay away from. If you go against what I'm about tell you, you may need more than this book to gain wealth as you may end up in a hole that is too deep to recover from.

Call Options

A call option can be your best friend, but if used the wrong way, it can quickly become the greatest enemy that you ever had. A call option gives the owner of it the right to purchase (call) a specific stock at a certain price (strike price) without regard to the current value.

For example, if I own a call option on Nike stock with a strike price of $30 and the stock rises to $100, the person who sold me the call would be forced to sell me the stock for $30 even though it is now worth $100 per share. Obviously, this would give me a quick $70 per share profit without having much initial risk since I only paid pennies on the dollar for the option to buy instead of buying the stock outright.

On the other hand, the person who sold me the call option would be in a deep world of mess. If he owned enough shares of the stock to satisfy my order, he could just sell me his shares, but if not, then he would have to buy the shares at the current market price of $100 per share and then turn around and sell them to me for only $30 per share.

This could obviously put him in a horrible situation, and one that I don't ever want any of my readers to be in because it could turn out much worse than this. What if the stock price went up to $2,000 per share? The person who sold me the option would have to go out and buy enough shares to satisfy my request at the market price of $2,000 per share and then sell them to me at $30 and lose a ton of money in the process.

If the person owned the shares that he sold me the option on, instead of being forced to buy the shares at market price, he would lose out on what could have been a magnificent profit since he would have to sell me his shares at only $30 instead of being able to sell them at the current market price of $2,000 per share.

Like I said, a call option could be your best friend if used properly, so it is important that you understand how to use one. For example, let's imagine that you've been watching a certain company's stock and you believe it is getting ready for a strong upturn but you're not sure.

Instead of buying 1,000 shares of the company's stock, which would be an expensive investment and a large risk, you could buy

10 call options (each option contract gives you the option to purchase 100 shares) that would give you the right to buy 1,000 shares at a specified price, so you can still profit from the stock's price gain (if it actually does increase) without having to actually own the shares at the time of the increase.

Put Option

Similar to a call option, if purchased, a put option could be your best friend and used like an insurance policy for a stock that you currently own to protect yourself against a downturn. A put option gives the owner of a stock the right to sell (put) a stock to the seller of the put option at a specified price, no matter what the actual stock price is at the time. For example, let's say I buy 100 shares of Walmart stock at $50 per share. If for some reason the stock price declined to $0, I would be at a loss of $5,000 unless I bought some insurance.

If, in this scenario, I purchased a put option with a strike price (right to sell price) of $50 immediately after I bought the stock and then the stock price declined to $0, I would still be able to sell my shares to the seller of the put option for $50 per share; therefore, my only loss would be the price that I paid for the put option.

In this scenario, the seller of the put option would be the one out of $5,000 minus the small revenue that he received from selling me the put option, which would probably only be around $500; therefore, the seller of the put option would have a net loss of $4,500, and I would have a loss of only $500.

As you can tell, buying a put option for protection is a great idea, while selling a put option to someone else can be a natural disaster waiting to happen. The thought of being forced to buy a stock for $50 that's no longer worth anything should show you the seriousness and potential dangers of selling put options.

Like with any investment, options can be good or bad depending on the level of knowledge of the investor. Also, one last note for selling call options is that they are particularly extra risky because there's no limit to how high a stock price can go, which gives the seller of the call an infinite amount of risk.

Retirement Accounts for Individual Investors

There are many options for an individual investor when selecting a retirement account, and I think that an investor should seek the assistance of a tax professional when preparing to open any type of retirement account. I think that using a qualified retirement account is ideal for most small investors, and the following accounts are a few that I think are worth consideration.

Traditional IRA

A traditional IRA permits an investor to deduct, from taxable income, contributions of up to the lesser amount of $5,500 ($6,500 if age 50 or older) or an investor's taxable compensation for the year. The contribution limits are for 2014 and will likely be adjusted for 2015. Traditional IRA contributions are considered above-the-line deductions and may be taken whether an investor itemizes or accepts the standard deduction.

You can withdraw money from a traditional IRA at any time. Distributions from traditional IRAs are taxed as ordinary income, and withdrawals that are made prior to becoming age 59½ are assessed an additional 10% penalty. There is a rule, however, that permits an investor to make tax-free withdrawals of contributions if the investor withdraws his contribution before the due date of his tax return for the same year that the contribution was made. In addition, there are several other ways to avoid the 10% additional tax penalty, which include using the funds to purchase a first home and having unreimbursed medical expenses that exceed 7.5% of your adjusted gross income.

Roth IRA

I generally prefer the Roth IRA over the traditional IRA. Although contributions to a Roth IRA cannot be deducted from taxable income, the earnings and interest grow tax free and withdrawals that are made after age 59½ are tax free on accounts that have been open for at least five years. Another benefit of a Roth IRA is that an investor can withdraw his contribution at any time without paying any taxes or penalties.

The contribution limits of a Roth IRA are identical to those of a traditional IRA, but there are more income restrictions that apply to Roth IRA contributors. Similar to traditional IRAs, there is a 10% penalty for making nonqualified withdrawals from a Roth IRA. With a Roth IRA, this penalty doesn't apply when withdrawing your original contributions, which can be withdrawn by an investor at any time without being taxed or penalized.

A qualified withdrawal is made from a Roth IRA if five years have passed since you set up and first funded your account and you must be either age 59½ or older, disabled, deceased and the payment is made to a beneficiary or to your estate, or you must use the funds to purchase what the IRS considers a first home. To satisfy the definition of first home, a person can't have an interest in a main home for the two-year period preceding the purchase of the new home.

If you have five years to wait and don't exceed the income limitations, I think a Roth IRA is a great savings tool for your first home. There is, however, a $10,000 limit currently on the amount that can be used from either a Roth or traditional IRA to aid in covering the expenses related to the purchase of a first home.

A good strategy is to have both a Roth and a traditional IRA. In years where an investor's income disqualifies him from investing into the Roth IRA, he has the option to invest the maximum amount into a traditional IRA.

Traditional 401(k)

Similar to a traditional IRA, a 401(k) allows an investor to defer some of his earnings and pay taxes on the income after retirement. Many employers offer 401(k) retirement plans for their employees, and I think that most employees would be wise to utilize the plans, especially if the employer makes a matching contribution. Employers that contribute to their employee's 401(k) plans often offer matching contributions that are subject to a vesting schedule, which means that the employer's contributions don't fully belong to the employee until after a pre-determined amount of time has expired.

In 2014, an employee can defer up to the lesser amount of 100% of his compensation or $17,500 with a 401(k), and a total amount of $52,000, including employer contributions, may be made annually to a 401(k). Similar to other retirement accounts, there is a 10% penalty for withdrawals that are taken prior to age 59½. Many 401(k) plans allow the participants to borrow money from their accounts, which generally must be repaid within five years to avoid taxes and penalties. If an employee leaves an employer, he can roll the assets from the 401(k) into a traditional IRA or his new employer's 401(k) plan without taxes or penalties.

Solo 401(k)

A solo 401(k) is for a self-employed individual or an owner of a very small business that has no employees. A self-employed person may invest as an employee and also add to his contributions as his own employer. A solo 401(k) is a very useful retirement plan and has the same rules and requirements as a traditional 401(k).

Last Words

As I stated earlier in the chapter, investing in stocks can be a very important piece of a well put together investment plan if used properly. They say knowledge is power, and with the information that you learned in this chapter, you should be prepared to make some great investments. Just remember to do more thinking than feeling, and you should be all right.

Chapter 7

10 Tips for Long-Term Stock Investing

Although everyday investors, due to the power of leverage, have the ability to create wealth much faster investing in real estate, a lot of money can also be created investing in stocks. However, an investor must have a game plan. Different rules apply when investing in stocks rather than trading stocks, and the following is a short list of tips to make long-term stock investing a success.

1. Only Buy Companies that You Expect to Remain Successful 10 Years after Investment

When investing in stocks for the long term, I only buy companies that I expect to be viable and strong 10 years after investment. Many businesses operate in industries that have futures that are hard to predict or technologies that may soon become outdated. I tend to stay away from companies that I don't believe will have a strong market presence 10 years after investment. When evaluating the long-term viability of a company, a lot of time is spent studying the company's business model and the expected growth of the company's industry.

2. Perform Due Diligence Before Making Every Investment

Regardless of how excited you become about a potential investment opportunity, it is extremely important to perform your due diligence before completing the transaction. During my typical due diligence session, I consider the viability of the company's business model, evaluate its valuation, including expected revenue and earnings growth, and I try to get a good feel for the company's top executives. I also read any recent earnings reports, material press releases, and third-party observations about the company. When researching third-party articles about the business, it is important to search for both positive and negative articles.

Although I will not purchase a company that is currently on a downward trend, I tend to not focus on the technicals as much as I do the fundamentals. Most of my time during due diligence is spent studying the company's valuation, management team, and researching information that supports its expected growth rate.

3. Invest in Companies with Strong Expected Revenue Growth

Although it is important to invest in companies that have the potential for strong earnings growth, I care a lot more about companies with strong revenue growth. Many companies are able to increase their earnings by cutting expenses, which is a good thing in business. However, I'm generally only impressed with companies that increase profits by increasing sales. A company can only cut expenses for so long before that approach is no longer an effective method to increase profits.

4. Invest in Companies that Have CEOs who Care About the Stock Price

I learned from Warren Buffett that an investor should always be confident in the prospective company's management team before making an investment. The ideal CEO is a visionary, who is a good manager of people and systems. The ideal CEO is also great at managing the confidence of investors and the expectations of Wall Street analysts.

If you don't know much about a particular CEO, it's a good idea to Google him or her and to find out as much information about him or her as possible. After collecting a sufficient amount of information about the prospective CEO, I try to determine if the executive has the desire and ability to manage the expectations of analysts and to excite investors, both of which will generally benefit the company's stock price.

5. Allocate at Least 25% of Your Portfolio to Income Producing Assets and Reinvest the Dividends

I try to allocate at least 25% of my portfolio to stocks that have a strong history of both paying and increasing dividends. Income is important for every portfolio, and the exact allocation should be based on how close you are to retirement and the amount of income that you receive from your other investments. A person who is in retirement or a person that is approaching retirement should allocate a much higher portion of his portfolio, possibly as much as 50%, to income producing stocks.

I tend to seek the majority of my income from business development companies and real estate investment trusts, both of which have a history of paying relatively large dividends to its shareholders. Many investors seek income from health care stocks and other defensively positioned companies that offer solid dividend payments. Regardless of which vehicles you choose for income, it is a good habit to reinvest the dividends to buy additional shares if you are not in retirement and don't need the funds to support everyday expenses. Reinvesting dividends can have a significant impact on your total return and is one of the better habits to have when long-term investing. Many investors enroll in dividend reinvestment plans with their brokerage firms, which allow investors to use cash dividend payments to buy additional shares of the dividend paying stock without paying a fee.

6. Buy Blocks of as Many Quality Companies, with Good Valuations, as Possible

Depending on the income and net worth of the individual investor, he should seek to invest a specific amount, at select intervals, into as many quality companies as possible. For example, a good strategy would be to invest $5,000 into a different company every three months or as your income allows. As the investor's financial situation improves, he should increase the size of his purchases.

I do, however, advise an investor to never own more companies than he can effectively manage. When the need to consolidate arises, an investor should consider either adding to current positions or selling the smaller blocks and using the funds to purchase larger blocks.

7. Pretend that You're a Private Equity Fund Manager when Selecting Stocks

Even though you are only buying relatively small blocks of stocks, treat it as if you're a private equity fund manager and that you're buying whole companies. It's important to know that you're buying companies when investing in stocks, which will likely cause you to become more discerning with the stocks that you choose.

8. Don't Fight the Fed

Both investors and traders need to keep a close watch on the Federal Reserve. When the FOMC is implementing policies that are meant to stimulate economic growth or increase inflation, stocks will likely flourish. In situations where an investor is unable to follow economic reports on a regular basis, lending an ear to the Fed will provide some helpful information about the future of its policies, which almost always have an impact on the stock market. For example, it would be less than prudent for a trader to short the stock market as a whole after hearing the Fed announce that it will empty its toolbox in an effort to promote economic growth. It would also be less than prudent not to reduce your level of exposure to the stock market after hearing from the Fed that it will take action to fight inflation or bubbles in stock or real estate markets.

9. Be Greedy When Others are Fearful

One of the best tips that I can share with long-term investors is to always have dry gun powder ready for the next recession. Stocks almost always go on sale during recessions, and this period of time usually offers one of the better entry points for buying and holding, which is a motto of long-term investors.

10. Unless You Have a Desperate Need for Capital, Never Sell a Good Company at a Bad Valuation— Wait Until the Market is Offering a Fair Price

There are many reasons as to why an investor should treat every stock purchase that he makes as a purchase of the whole company. One of the main reasons that this is good practice is because, during downturns in the market, investors will be less likely to sell good companies at depressed valuations. Many amateur investors buy stocks at high prices and then get nervous and sell at lower valuations when the market changes directions. Treating every stock that you own as a company that you own will change your prospective on selling during recessions and troughs.

Last Words

The world of stock investing is a wonderful place to explore. However, it is important that no investments are made hastily and that due diligence is completed before buying any stock, regardless of its potential for growth or relatively large dividends.

Chapter 8

Investing in Bonds

I'm not a big fan of bonds for active and knowledgeable investors on their way to wealth, and I believe that they are much better for established individuals and bond traders. However, I don't want to confuse anyone into thinking that they are bad investments because that's not the case. I just don't think that they make good investments for those who are not already established.

What Are Bonds?

A bond, which may be referred to as a note or bill depending on its length, is a contract between the issuer and the investor. The investor loans money to the issuer, which can be a corporation, the United States government, or a municipal board. In return for borrowing your money to the issuer, it agrees to pay you a fixed amount of money, which is usually based on a percentage, for a certain period of time before it gives you your money back.

For example, let's say that Karen bought a Walmart bond with a face value of $5,000 (or five bonds in $1,000 increments) that pays her 5% a year for seven years. In reality, she loaned Walmart $5,000 for seven years, and Walmart is going to pay her a 5% yield each year for seven years. Each year for seven years, Walmart will pay her $250 (5% of $5,000) until the end of the seven-year period, and that's when Walmart will pay her back the original $5,000 that she loaned the company.

This picture does look a little better when considering much larger dollar amounts as shown in the next example. Let's say that

Karen won the lottery and bought $5 million in bonds from General Motors. Let's also say that with all of the trouble that the company has had over the last decade, it has to pay investors much higher yields to compensate for the risk, and GM gave her a 9% yield on a seven-year bond. In this scenario, GM would pay her $450,000 (9% of $5 million) a year for seven years.

My strong opinion, which appears to be a dislike for bonds, is mainly geared toward investing small dollar amounts in them like the first scenario of Karen and only getting so little in return. I would advise someone with only $5,000 to invest in equities or to start a small business.

Par Value of a Bond

The par value, which is also used interchangeably with face value, of a bond is the amount that will be paid to the investor when the bond matures. This amount is usually the same amount that was originally borrowed to the issuer by the investor but can be different depending on the terms of agreement.

For example, let's say that Karen bought a five-year, $1,000 bond from Exxon Mobil with a 5% yield. In addition to the $50 (5% of $1,000) a year that she would receive from Exxon Mobile, at the end of the five years Karen would then receive her $1,000 in full that she originally borrowed Exxon Mobil. That $1,000 would be considered the par or face value.

Premiums & Discounts

Just as stocks can be traded, so can bonds. Also, just as the price that you sell a stock for may be different from the price that you paid, so can be the case when selling bonds.

Not all bonds that are issued are held to maturity (the end of the loan period). In fact, many of them are sold on the secondary market at either a premium or at a discount years before the maturity date.

When a bond sells at a premium, it is sold for more than the par or face value of the loan. For example, a $1,000 bond selling at a premium might sell for $1,100. Bonds are generally sold at a premium if the bond has a higher interest rate or yield than what is currently being offered on the market.

For example, If Karen purchases a $1,000 bond with a yield of 8% when interest rates are high, and then a year later the best rate being offered for new bonds is 5%, Karen would be able to sell her bond at a premium as it is paying a higher interest rate or yield than what is currently being offered on the market.

On the flip side of the token, a bond could also be sold at a discount. When a bond sells at a discount, it is sold for less than the par value of the loan. Bonds are usually sold at a discount when the yield on it is less than what is currently being sold on the market.

For example, let's say Karen purchases a $1,000 bond with a yield of 4%, and nine months later, the interest rate being offered for that bond is 7%. If Karen wanted to sell her bond before the maturity date, she would have to sell it for less than the face value as not too many people will want to buy a 4% bond for the same price that they can buy a 7% bond. It wouldn't make sense. She would probably end up selling her bond for a lot less than $1,000 since the 3% difference in her bond's interest rate and what the market is currently offering would cause for her to take a deep discount.

Bond Ratings

When investing, the reward of the investor is generally determined by the level of risk that is assumed. The higher the risk, the higher the potential reward must be and vice versa. If there is little risk for the investor, the investor generally gets little reward. This is true with most investments and bonds are no exception.

The amount of risk that the investor assumes when loaning a company or government entity money will determine the interest rate given with the bond. If the company that is issuing the bond has had losses over the last couple quarters, its bonds are considered riskier and must give higher yields to compensate for the high amount of risk.

On the other hand, if the U.S. government is issuing the bond, there is very little risk assumed by the investor as it is considered the most stable entity in the world. In this case, the investor would have to accept a below average interest rate since there is very little risk involved. However, it is critically important to understand that when interest rates are at or near historic lows, bonds are at great risk due to the fact that interest rates will eventually normalize and interest rate increases are often disastrous for bond holders.

To help investors measure the amount of risk associated with each bond, Moody's and Standard & Poor's are two very prominent companies that rate the quality of each company's bond.

These two companies generally divide the risk of each bond between investment grade and speculative. Obviously, the investment grade bonds have the lower interest rates, and the junk bonds have much higher interest rates to compensate for the additional risk.

With Moody's, the best grade that is given for the highest quality bond is Aaa, and then it proceeds with Aa, A, and Baa for investment grade bonds. Its junk bonds proceed in the following order: Ba, B, Caa, Ca, and C. The lower the grade, the higher the yield must be to attract investors.

With Standard and Poor's, the bond grades from best quality to worst are AAA, AA, A, BBB, and BBB- for investment grade, and BB+, BB, B, CCC, CC, C, and D for junk bonds. Since they carry much higher interest rates than investment grade bonds, junk bonds are often called high-yield bonds.

How to Purchase

Although most bonds don't trade on exchanges like stocks, they are fairly easy to purchase. Most bond transactions are performed in the over-the-counter market, which means they are between two private parties without the aid or supervision of an exchange. Many bond buyers use online brokers, such as TDAmeritrade. Others, who only invest in government bonds, purchase them directly from the government at TreasuryDirect.gov.

It is important to know that many brokers will apply a mark up to the bond price, which is fair game as long as the mark up is reasonable. An investor in bonds shouldn't pay more than a 2% premium for any bond purchase, so it is important to have a discussion with your broker regarding any potential mark up.

Last Words

When this chapter first started, it may have appeared that I was anti-bonds. The truth is that I am not anti-bonds, but I did make it appear that way intentionally. That is because there are much better things to do with your money if you have limited resources. Investing in bonds is not for a poor or middle class person as it will only help him stay poor or middle class.

On the other hand, if you are rich and want to live off of assets, I think bonds may make a very good investment for you if you're investing at least $2 million and receiving a minimum of a 5% yield. This way, you know to expect $100,000 a year for the life of the bond, and then you can expect to receive your $2 million at the end of the life of the bond.

Like I said before, investment choices should be decided considering all factors, including, but not limited to, your investment goals, risk tolerance, ambition, and investment knowledge.

Chapter 9

Business Entities

Besides the investing techniques discussed in earlier chapters, there are many other legitimate ways to build wealth in this country, and the most famous strategy is by starting your own business. Not everyone is willing take this risk as the level of risk is directly correlated to the high potential for reward.

In fact, the definition of entrepreneur describes someone who takes a risk and starts a business. Therefore, it isn't a secret that there is a big risk starting a business, and it also isn't a secret that many of the richest men in the world are entrepreneurs, including Bill Gates with Microsoft.

As I stated in an earlier chapter, I believe that the level of risk associated with something all depends on the level of knowledge the investor has in that particular business or investment. For example, if the founder of Nike decided to start another shoe company, it wouldn't be very much of a risk to him since he has the experience from building one of the largest shoe companies in the world. While at the same time, if he tried to start a hair salon franchise, it would be much more risk associated for him as his experience level on this topic is likely to be slim to none.

Starting and building a successful business can be one of the most rewarding feelings that a person can ever experience. Building a profitable business gives a person great feeling of accomplishment and wealth that can be passed down from generation to generation.

However, all of this potential for reward does come with an equal amount of risk and a large potential for failure. More than half of small businesses fail within the first five years. This can be a very intimidating number to some people, while being used as motivation for others.

The chance for failure can be dramatically decreased with proper preparation before starting a business by doing research, shadowing other professionals in the industry, and definitely by reading all that you can. I was taught when I was younger that proper preparation prevents poor performance. With this in mind, it is scary to think of all of the people out there who start a business without putting together a sound business plan.

Another thing that many entrepreneurs fail to do is select the appropriate business entity for their type of business. This may not sound very serious, but it definitely is something that deserves high ranking on an entrepreneur's priority list. Certain entities will protect your personal assets, such as your house and savings, while starting a business with other entities will put many of your personal possessions at risk in the event something goes wrong financially involving your business.

Selecting the appropriate entity is very important when attempting to build a successful business. Besides completing a strong business plan, which outlines your choice of entity anyway, I believe that carefully selecting the appropriate entity is the most important thing for any entrepreneur.

In today's litigious society, there are thousands of lawsuits being filed daily. Some of these lawsuits are legitimate, while many of them are people just trying to get rich with a phony claim. Some of these lawsuits are being filed against the actual owners of the businesses, while many others, due to the choice of entity by the entrepreneur, are filed against the business only, and the plaintiff can't go after any of the entrepreneur's personal belongings.

A person's wife is not likely to understand why the family has to lose personal property because of a lawsuit brought forth due to an act of negligence done by one of her husband's employees. Although this sounds horrifying, it happens often and mainly because of a failure to perform key acts of due diligence, which is often due to a lack of patience.

Sometimes when a person wants to make money, he loses sight of everything else that he is involved in or becomes very limited in what he sees. This is especially the case with young entrepreneurs who have created a very good product or who have come up with a brilliant plan. After the concept of the business has been created, the entrepreneur will often see only dollars signs and the potential profits of the idea.

This causes many entrepreneurs to lose sight of some of the most important things when starting a business, such as putting together a solid business plan and selecting the appropriate entity. When doing these two things correctly, it definitely increases the entrepreneur's chance for success.

To help make you aware of your entity options, I will give you a list and details of the most popular entity choices available, such as the C corporation, S corporation, limited liability company, limited partnership, limited liability partnership, limited liability limited partnership, general partnership, and the sole proprietorship.

C Corporation

What does Walmart, Home Depot, Nike, McDonald's, Microsoft, and just about every other company traded on the New York Stock Exchange and NASDAQ have in common? The answer is that they are all C corporations.

C corporations are the most popular entity for large businesses and small businesses that plan to become large and publicly traded companies. C corporations have many benefits, but a C corporation is not for every business as some businesses will serve better as either a limited liability company or S corporation.

One of the advantages of a C corporation over all other entities is that the ownership interests are easily exchanged, which is huge for raising capital or providing an alternative payment method to employees. This is the main reason why all of the large companies that I named above that are traded on the stock market are C corporations.

A C corporation is considered its own separate entity and can do many things that a person can, such as buy real estate, buy other businesses, get credit cards, sue people, and at the same time be sued.

Limited Liability

One of the best things about a C corporation is that it provides limited liability to its shareholders. This means that the only risk an investor has when investing in a C corporation is the investment that he makes into the business. This limited liability is not, however, absolute. Generally, the owner of a C corporation cannot be personally sued for the negligent acts of the business' employees or for debts of the business unless the owner has agreed to be held personally liable.

Due to the limited liability factor, in the event of a lawsuit, the corporation is the proper defendant, not the actual owners of the business. This adds a great level of protection. Some entities, however, allow all of the owners to be held liable for any liabilities of the business and the owners can be sued for personal belongings, such as their homes, cars, and life savings to make right for wrongdoings or debts of the business.

Beware of Torts

It is critically important to know that, regardless of your business entity, a person is always responsible for his own torts, which are wrongful acts. The most common tort is negligence. The elements of negligence are duty, breach, causation, and damages. Determining if a duty was owed in a particular situation is a question of law and is the job of the court (judge). Determining if there was a breach of that duty is a question of fact that is answered by the jury.

An example of being negligent would be a self-employed cab driver running a red light and injuring a pedestrian with his vehicle. Although he may have operated as a corporation or as an LLC, the driver would still be personally liable in addition to the company that he owns. Even if the driver isn't the owner of the cab company, both he and the company will generally be held liable. When a tort is committed by an employee within the course and scope of employment, the tortfeasor is liable because he committed the tort and the employer is liable based on the legal concept of respondeat superior.

Another example of being negligent would be not performing a reasonable amount of due diligence before hiring someone. Many courts, including in Texas, have ruled that employers have a legal duty to the public and other employees to exercise ordinary care when hiring.

It is also possible to negligently train, retain, and supervise someone. The legal theories of negligent hiring, training, retaining, and supervising are usually brought forth when the tortfeasor was acting outside the course and scope of employment when he committed the tort.

The benefits of limited liability are that you are not responsible for the torts of others simply because you own or manage an entity and, unless he provides a personal guarantee, the holder of limited liability is generally not responsible for contracts and other debts of the business.

Piercing the Corporate Veil

In some instances, the limited liability of a corporation and its owners can be disregarded. When the limited liability aspect of a corporation is disregarded, it is legally called piercing the corporate veil. Piercing the corporate veil means that an owner or executive of a corporation is being held personally liable for the actions or debts of the business. This generally only happens in situations where corporate formalities are ignored or when the owners or executives have committed an act of fraud.

Actions that can cause the allowance of piercing the corporate veil would include the owner commingling business and personal funds, deceiving someone into doing business with the corporation while thinking he is doing business with a person, and fraud. These are all common reasons that will allow piercing of the corporate veil and remove an owner's right to limited liability.

Fraud

Since it is a potential trap for entrepreneurs and executives, I will briefly discuss the basic elements of fraud. Fraud has five elements, which include intentionally making a statement that is known to be false with the intent that the other party rely on such statement and the reliance of the statement by the other party causes his detriment. It is also possible to commit fraud by concealing material facts; therefore, just because you don't say anything, it doesn't mean that you haven't committed fraud, especially if there was a clear duty to speak.

Fiduciary Duties

The board of directors owe two very important duties to the corporation: the duty of care and the duty of loyalty. The duty of care requires that directors exercise care when making business decisions and courts generally apply the business judgment rule when determining if a director breached his duty of care. The business judgment rule considers if the director acted as a reasonable person would after an adequate amount of due diligence.

The duty of loyalty requires members of the board to act in good faith and in the best interest of the corporation. It is strongly advised that directors not make business deals with the corporation unless it is clearly in the best interest of the business and the transaction is approved by a majority of disinterested members of the board.

Taxation

As its own entity, a corporation must file its own tax return separately of the individual owners. Opposite of other limited liability entities, if a corporation takes a loss for the year it cannot pass that loss down to the company's owners and is only considered a loss for the business. Businesses that can pass down losses are considered pass-through entities, and the C corporation is not one of them. An owner of a pass-through entity pays taxes at the owner's individual tax rate.

One of the other downsides to the way corporations are taxed is the fact that they are often double taxed. What double taxation means is that a corporation must pay taxes on any profits it earns, and if the company decides to pay out any dividends to its owners, they will also be taxed on their share of profits received, therefore, causing double taxation.

This is very unfavorable among many entrepreneurs and is the reason why many of them stray away from C corporations until they are ready to go public or seek private capital. It is important to note that a business can start out as one entity and then switch to another with the filing of a certificate of conversion.

Forming a C Corporation

A C corporation is formed by filing what is known as the articles of incorporation with the secretary of state. In Texas, the proper name is certificate of formation. The articles of incorporation would include the entity's name, registered agent information, a list of the board of directors, the number of authorized shares, purpose, and duration of the business. Depending on the state, more or less information may be required.

The bylaws of a corporation outline the rules of the business and how management is to handle corporate affairs, such as shareholder and board meetings. The bylaws also generally include the proper procedure to remove directors and executives from office.

Each state charges a different fee for filing the articles of incorporation, so it's important to get those numbers ahead of time from your local secretary of state's office.

A resident agent must be designated in the state that the corporation is organized. The role of the resident agent is to accept lawsuits in case they are ever filed against your business. The owner of a corporation can serve as his own resident agent if he lives in the state that the business is formed; otherwise, an attorney is always a good option.

Close Corporation

Generally, a corporation must designate at least one person as a board member when starting a corporation. However, a close corporation, which typically has fewer than 50 shareholders and restrictions on stock transfers, may be managed by a shareholders' agreement instead of having a formal board of directors. Close corporations often have to adhere to less corporate formalities than traditional corporations. To form a close corporation in Texas, the certificate of formation or the certificate of amendment must state that it is a close corporation.

S Corporation

The S corporation is very similar to the C corporation. In fact, in order to have an S corporation, one must form a C corporation first. After incorporating into a C corporation, the business owner must then file form 2553 with the IRS in order to qualify for S corporation status.

As with a C corporation, an S corporation also has limited liability protection from debts and wrongdoings of the business and its employees. The differences between an S corporation and a C corporation are noticed within its tax status and restrictions.

Tax Status

An S corporation is considered a pass-through tax entity. This means that only the owners of an S corporation pay taxes on profits, which is opposite of a C corporation where the business has to file its own tax return and pay taxes on any profits.

All profits or losses of an S corporation pass down to its owners. This means that if the business takes a loss, actual or only on paper, the loss passes down to the owner's personal tax return. For example, let's say Lisa started a part-time business and formed it as an S corporation that had a loss of $50,000 its first year. Let's also say that

Lisa still had her full-time job as an engineer that paid her $60,000 a year. Because of the pass-through tax status of an S corporation, after deducting the $50,000 business loss from her $60,000 salary as an engineer, she would only pay taxes on $10,000 of income as that would be her new adjusted gross income, minus or plus any other income or deductions. It is important to check with your tax consultant as there are often time and monetary restrictions on the amount of losses that can be deducted from personal income.

This is a good reason to form an S corporation instead of a C corporation as this is not allowed with a C corporation. A loss with a C corporation is considered a loss of the business that cannot be passed down to its owners.

S Corporation Restrictions

The S corporation has several restrictions that make it unattractive depending on the goals of the business and the way it is to be owned and controlled. The following are a few guidelines that may lead a person to form a C corporation or a limited liability company instead of an S corporation.

1.) S corporations are not permitted to have more than 100 shareholders. This is one of the reasons a large business that has the intentions to go public should not form an S corporation since most publicly traded companies have millions or billions of shares available to the public to be traded.

2.) Corporations and many types of trusts may not be shareholders of an S corporation. This is another reason why a large company that plans to go public should not form an S corporation. A large public company's stock is usually purchased by other corporations but cannot be if it's an

S corporation. However, 501(c)(3) non-profit corporations are allowed to be shareholders.

3.) An S corporation may not have non-U.S. citizens as shareholders. This is another tough restriction of an S corporation since venture capitalists, angels, and other potential investors may actually be residents of another country.

4.) An S corporation may only have one class of stock. It cannot have preferred and common stock. This is another pitfall of the S corporation as some investors will want to receive a different class of stock than the other investors but will be unable to do so in an S corporation since only one form of stock is allowed.

5.) Profits and losses of an S corporation must be split evenly based on the percentage of ownership. This means that if one of the owners owns 20% of the business, he can only receive 20% of the profits or losses of the company.

Limited Liability Company (LLC)

In my opinion, the limited liability company (LLC) is the best of both worlds. Out of all the entities it is my favorite one by far. Generally, the only time that I wouldn't use a limited liability company is if I were getting ready to take a business public.

The limited liability company has the limited liability protection of the C and S corporations and the pass-through tax status of the S corporation without all of the crazy restrictions, giving it the best of both worlds. The biggest difference between a limited liability company and an S corporation is the way that profits and losses can be divided.

As stated above, in an S corporation, the profits and losses must be divided evenly based on the percentage of ownership. For example, if Kate and Michael equally own an S corporation, they must split the profits or losses of the business 50/50. No other agreement would be legal even if in writing.

With a limited liability company, the profits and losses can be distributed in any way that the owners please. Therefore, if a particular investor will only invest if he gets 50% of the profits for the first two years, but he only owns 25% of the business, with a limited liability company this is perfectly attainable as long as it's agreed to in writing. This is a big advantage over the S corporation in addition to the lack of restrictions that are applied to the limited liability company.

Forming a Limited Liability Company

In order to form a limited liability company, one must file the articles of organization with the secretary of state. There is a fee to file this and it varies by state. The articles of organization include the company's name, purpose, duration, resident agent, and if the business is to be manager or member managed. Depending on the state, more or less information may be required.

With an LLC, member managed means that all owners will have executive power over the business and manager managed means that a separate person or group of people, who may or may not also be members, will have executive power over the business.

The next form that must be put together, although not filed with the secretary of state, is the company's operating agreement. The operating agreement outlines the rules for operating the business. It will generally list requirements for meetings, removing managers, process to transfer or sell ownership interests, and distribution of profits and losses. If the last part isn't included, profits and losses must be divided according to ownership percentages.

The limited liability company has a lot of benefits and can be the perfect entity depending on the goals and objectives of the business and its owners. Like I stated before, unless I plan on going public in the near future, the LLC is my business entity of choice.

Series LLC

Some states offer what is known as a series LLC, which allows for an LLC to provide in its governing documents the establishment of a series of members, managers, membership interests, or assets that have separate rights, liabilities, and business purposes from the general LLC. Series LLCs are very valuable to real estate investors as they may be formed and used to hold, but keep separate, real estate investments for liability purposes.

For example, an owner of a series LLC may place an investment property into one of the series and another property into another series. Properly using a series LLC assures that if there is an obligation of one of the series, it will not become a liability of the general LLC or of any other series. In states where they are allowed, many investors use the series LLC as an alternative to forming a holding company with several subsidiaries.

Each series of a series LLC has the right to sue, be sued, make investments, and enter into contracts. There is a limited amount of case law concerning series LLCs; therefore, to increase the chances of properly using a series LLC, it is important to keep separate bank accounts for each series, sign contracts with a clear designation of a particular series, and make sure each series is properly capitalized. The issue of using a series LLC is something that should be discussed with both legal and tax professionals.

Limited Partnership

The limited partnership (LP) in my opinion is a half good and half bad entity. A limited partnership is a business that has at least one limited partner and at least one general partner. The reason I say that a limited partnership is half good and half bad is because only the limited partners have limited liability of personal risk, but the general partner is at total risk and is held personally responsible for any debts or wrongdoings of the business.

The general partner is the one who manages the business and has executive say over the business and its day-to-day operations. The general partner is usually the one who founded the business or in most cases was the primary investor. The general partners have no limited liability protection of personal assets and can be wiped clean if the business has a large lawsuit against it or debts that can't be paid with business assets.

The limited partner is considered a silent partner and has minimal say in the day-to-day decisions of the business. If a limited partner becomes too actively involved in the business, he can lose his limited liability protection since only a general partner has the right to be involved in the day-to-day management of a limited partnership.

The limited partner is usually a minority investor in the business and wants nothing to do with the operation of the business because he doesn't want to lose his limited liability protection.

One key strategy that many attorneys advise clients to use is to form a limited partnership with a separate LLC acting as the general partner. This strategy is useful for business owners who want to keep outside investors from becoming members of management and it also provides the general partner limited liability protection.

Forming a Limited Partnership

To form a limited partnership, you must file a certificate of limited partnership with the secretary of state. The certificate of limited partnership generally includes the partnership's name, resident agent information, principal office, and general partner information.

A limited partnership must also structure a limited partnership agreement. The limited partnership agreement generally lists the duties of the general partner, the limited partners' voting rights, division of ownership interests, and guidelines for transferring or selling ownership interests.

Limited Liability Partnership & Limited Liability Limited Partnership

Some states allow for the use of both limited liability partnerships (LLP) and limited liability limited partnerships (LLLP). It is important to note that registering a general partnership as an LLP or registering a limited partnership as an LLLP does not create a new entity. In some states, including in Texas, a limited liability partnership is a pre-existing general partnership that takes the additional step of registering with the secretary of state. Registering a general partnership as a limited liability partnership provides the general partners with some level of limited liability that is not normally afforded to general partners.

A limited liability limited partnership is a pre-existing limited partnership that takes the additional step of registering with the secretary of state to obtain some level of limited liability protection for its general partners.

General Partnership and Sole Proprietorship

A general partnership and a sole proprietorship are the most horrible business entities known to man when it comes to personal asset protection. A general partnership is a partnership with all general partners and no limited partners, which means that everyone involved in a general partnership is at risk of personal assets being seized to satisfy the debts of the business; therefore, no one in a general partnership is safe.

A sole proprietorship is a one-person owned business where the owner takes full personal liability for the business. With all the entity options available, I don't understand why people are still forming these two forms of business entities. In my personal opinion, a person should be committed for forming one of these, especially if there are plans for the business to enter into contracts or hire employees.

Forming a General Partnership & Sole Proprietorship

Any time you start a business without filing with the secretary of state for an entity that provides limited liability protection, you have automatically started a sole proprietorship. If the business is with at least one other person, you have automatically entered into a general partnership. I strongly advise against using either entity if the entrepreneur plans to enter into contracts on behalf of the business or if the business plans to have employees.

Last Words

When picking an entity for your business, it is important to choose one that will benefit your needs. Also, one must consider the need for tax breaks and deductions to personal income if the business is expected to take a loss.

Remember to never form a sole proprietorship or general partnership if you plan for the business to enter into contracts or hire employees. Keep in mind that if you start a business with another person and haven't filed for a specific entity, you have automatically started a general partnership. Also, if you are starting a business by yourself and haven't filed for a specific entity, you have automatically started a sole proprietorship.

Chapter 10

Preparing Business Plans: The Algorithm for Success

The rate at which small businesses fail can be an alarming number since small businesses are responsible for creating the majority of all new jobs. There are many reasons as to why small businesses fail, including, but not limited to, ignoring the competition, ineffective marketing, ignoring consumer needs, incompetent employees, poor location, cash-flow problems, and a lack of leadership by example from the management staff.

Many entrepreneurs, when looking for a location to start their businesses, don't take into account such simple things as the area's traffic, which is vital to your success. You can have the best restaurant in the world, but if no one ever hears about it or drives near it, the business will likely fail within the first three to five years. Research shows that many people take more time to plan their vacations than they do to properly plan for their businesses, which is scary.

Also, an abundance of entrepreneurs don't take into account what the consumers in their areas want to buy that's not already being provided to them at prices that are lower than their businesses can afford to beat. This also goes in line with ignoring the competition.

Resources for Information

Completing a thorough business plan will force an entrepreneur to answer all of the questions that an entrepreneur knows that he must deal with and the questions that many times an entrepreneur wouldn't tend to even think to answer. When completing a business plan, it is imperative to have multiple resources available that can be used to accumulate key information, such as the size and expected growth of your industry and target market.

Online Tools

There are many online resources that can be used to help aid in the collection of data for the planning process. It is a good practice to keep track of where you find information. During the research phase of the planning process, it is likely that you will find a lot of information that will become useful to you when completing the actual details of your business plan. The following are websites that I believe are extremely helpful during the planning process:

1.) U.S. Census Bureau: www.census.gov – The U.S. Census Bureau's website, which is one of the most reliable sources of online information, has a plethora of useful information that you will need when researching key statistics for your business plan. The U.S. Census Bureau has important information about specific industries, states, cities, and neighborhoods. Before paying for any information, be sure to thoroughly exhaust the information available on the Census Bureau's website.

2.) The World Bank: www.worldbank.org – The World Bank, which is an international organization headquartered in Washington that focuses on reducing extreme poverty, is one of the most credible sources for international statistics. The World Bank's research tools are excellent for businesses with an international focus.

3.) Export.gov: www.export.gov – Export.gov is another useful tool for American businesses that seek to break into international markets. Export.gov, if used in conjunction with The World Bank's website, can provide the large majority of information that is required when planning to expand into overseas territories.

4.) National Association of Manufacturing: www.nam.org – The National Association of Manufacturing's website should be visited early and often in the planning process for manufacturers. The site hosts key information about manufacturing companies and the manufacturing industry as a whole.

5.) Thomas Register: www.thomasregister.com – Thomas Register is probably the best resource for finding suppliers. The website allows you to find suppliers by product category and is extremely helpful for manufacturing companies.

6.) Dun & Bradstreet: www.dnb.com – Although the company offers multiple business solutions, its website is a great place to find information on suppliers and competitors, including credit reports and financial information.

Other Sources

1.) Small Business Development Centers: Small Business Development Centers are located throughout the country and are a valuable source for entrepreneurs. Small Business Development Centers offer assistance with the business planning process, financing, manufacturing, exporting, and much more.

2.) SCORE: SCORE is probably the best source for finding a quality mentor to help guide you through the planning and execution of your business plan. Best of all, Score is a nonprofit organization that offers its services free of charge as a community service.

3.) Surveys: If you are having difficulty finding information that is required for the completion of your business plan, it may be necessary to conduct a survey. It is important to make sure that surveys are not too long and that they focus on the key issues that your business is facing.

4.) Focus Groups: In some situations, it may be better to turn a survey into a discussion in order to obtain highly constructive feedback. A typical focus group will be made up of a collection of people from a targeted group that discuss a key product or service. Focus groups allow entrepreneurs to gain a better understanding of their problems and are usually very insightful.

The Plan

Depending on the complexity of the business concept and its intended audience, a business plan should be between 10 and 35 pages, which does not include any appendices that should provide supplemental information to the plan. The planning process is often very lengthy and may take more than six months to complete. Unless an entrepreneur is able to budget for private consultants, he should seek assistance from a mentor from SCORE. The following are the sections that should be included in every business plan.

Executive Summary

The executive summary, which should be no more than three pages, is the most important part of a business plan and is usually the first and only section read by potential investors. An effective executive summary will create excitement by placing an emphasis on the most compelling details of the business plan. If the executive summary is not successful at creating excitement from the reader, the remaining sections of the plan are not likely to be read.

Although the executive summary appears at the beginning of a business plan, it should be the last section completed. A thorough and concise executive summary will cover details about the company's background, concept, target market, market trends, competitive advantages, management team, and key financial projections. In the event that the business plan is being used to solicit funding, the executive summary should also mention the amount of funds being sought and include a couple of paragraphs detailing any material headwinds or risks that may prevent success and key steps to overcome such obstacles.

It is important to not give in to the temptation of writing your executive summary first. Much of the information that should be included in the executive summary will not be available to you until you've finished the remaining sections of your plan.

Company Description

The objective of the company description is to communicate the most basic details of your business, such as its name, entity type, products or services, and its mission statement. The mission statement is probably the section of the company description that has the best chance of impressing readers. If written correctly, a strong mission statement will concisely describe the company's objectives and underlying principles.

The company description should also include details about the management team, location, and stage of development. The stage of development should describe if the company is a startup or an established business.

Industry Analysis

Many people often use the words *industry* and *sector* interchangeably. The economy is generally divided into 18 sectors, which are much larger than industries. For example, the finance and insurance sector can be broken into a plethora of industries, including asset management, credit services, and savings & loans.

Sectors and industries are both affected by the strength of the economy; however, the economy doesn't have the same impact on all industries. Some businesses actually perform better during economic downturns and knowing if your company is operating within an industry that grows inverse to the general economy is critically important while planning and executing your business plan.

The U.S. Census Bureau is my favorite resource for identifying trends within particular industries. It is wise to compare your industry's past and expected growth to the nation's gross domestic product. Although there are exceptions to almost every rule, it is prudent to focus on industries that have the potential to exceed the growth rate of the overall economy.

A solid industry analysis will provide sufficient information about the availability of suppliers and distributers and will identify the size of the industry, past and projected growth, typical profit margins, and a list of any headwinds that may be facing the industry, including any technological or regulatory changes.

Target Market

A company's target market can be described as the main group of people or institutions that the company plans to solicit, via advertising or other means, to do business with the company. Determining the size and expected growth of your target market is critically important during the planning process. Many investors will only invest into businesses that have target markets that are both well-defined and large enough to promote sustainable growth.

A well-defined target market may identify core customers by age, sex, marital status, location, interests, or income. It is important to make sure that your target market is neither too large nor too small. If a target market is too large, there may be many well-financed competitors in the market, and it may be hard to reach the targeted group with the typical marketing budget for small start-ups. Obviously, a target market that is too small will likely not have enough customers to support growth or entice investors.

Businesses that sell their products directly to retailers should be mindful of the characteristics of both the targeted retailers and the actual consumer. A business plan that doesn't take into consideration the challenges or headwinds presented with entering into retail outlets will likely be dismissed by potential investors.

Competition

A detailed analysis of the competition, especially competitors with a large share of the market, will provide an entrepreneur with some very helpful information about the industry and his potential customers. Having a good understanding of your competitors will also enable you to properly articulate the differences between what you and the competition have to offer.

It is never a good idea to assume that you have no competitors. If a potential investor notices something in your business plan that indicates that you believe that you have no competitors, neither the business plan nor the entrepreneur will be perceived as having much credibility. It is also important to thoroughly consider which companies may become competitors in the future.

Often times when a company is early entering into a market and proves that it can be successful, competitors will appear from both new and established companies. In such a case, be prepared to compete and differentiate. A good example of differentiating is a recent set of Microsoft commercials promoting its Windows 8 tablet. The commercials do an exceptional job of comparing its tablet computer to Apple's tablet computer. The commercials have the two tablets speaking to each other while the Windows 8 tablet performs functions that Apple's tablet are unable to perform. Although Apple was early into the tablet market and was able to define the product's standard features, Microsoft was able to study Apple as a competitor and offer features that were demanded by customers but were not offered by Apple's product.

When completing an analysis of the competition, it is important to describe any barriers that may prevent someone from entering the market and competing, such as patents or high startup costs. Investors are more likely to invest if there are obstacles, legal or financial, for a company to directly compete.

Strategic Position

The strategic positioning of a business takes into consideration what the company has learned from its competition and industry analysis to determine how to best compete for market share. Many entrepreneurs and executives often compete on the basis of price, quality, or both. It is of vital importance to not try to compete on the basis of price alone with most large companies, which benefit from economies of scale. Such companies can usually accept a loss and continue operating successfully for a much longer period of time than many smaller companies. Eventually, the smaller company, when competing with a much larger company on the basis of price alone, will go bankrupt and the larger competitor then has the ability to return to its normal pricing structure.

If you are introducing a new product or service to the market, there are several key benefits and risks that must be considered. Being first to market allows a business the opportunity to capture substantial market share and secure exclusive relationships with key strategic partners, such as suppliers, manufacturers, and distributors. On the other hand, being first to market also has its risks, including not being embraced by the market and significant research & development costs.

Marketing & Sales

Your marketing & sales plan will detail how the company plans to make the target market aware of what the company has to offer and how the company will make sales. It is the job of the marketing department to make life easier for the sales team. Sales teams that are supported by strong marketing campaigns are much more likely to be successful than sales teams that retain the duty of creating brand awareness. Many companies hire advertising agencies for planning and execution of marketing plans, which I think increases the likelihood of conveying the intended and correct message to the target market.

A good marketing plan will detail the cost and expected efficacy of the marketing vehicles that will be utilized to reach the market, such as online advertising, print media, and television placements. The marketing & sales plan should also provide details about the sales force, including compensation, responsibilities, and sales processes.

Operations

The operations section of a business plan describes the day-to-day functions of the business and provides information about the company's location, facilities, equipment, production processes, quality control, inventory system, supply chain, and research & development.

In my opinion, the quality control portion is the most important part of the operations section. It is very critical to have processes in place to identify and address customer concerns before they become past customers. It is very common for unhappy customers to neither complain nor return. Every business should perpetually solicit feedback from its customers and take action based on its findings.

While some companies limit their quality control efforts to simply requesting that customers complete feedback forms, some companies hire consultants to implement quality management systems, such as ISO 9001.

Technology

The technology section of a solid business plan will demonstrate that the entrepreneur is aware of his current and future technology needs. It is wise to not select software and hardware based on cost alone. Technology selections should also be based on functionality and flexibility.

Just about every business uses some sort of technology. Even a small business without much of a need for technology will still likely need a computer, accounting software, and a business phone. The recent emergence of cloud computing, however, has reduced the costs associated with purchasing software.

Management

The management section should be concise and describe the organizational structure and key members of management that are vital to the company's success. The plan should include enough relevant information about the management team that readers are confident that the management team has the ability to successfully execute the plan. Investors understand that a great business plan is worthless if it can't be properly executed.

For corporations, it is advised to solicit professionals with relevant industry experience to become members of the board of directors. Having a board of directors with a plethora of experience can often encourage investors to take a leap of faith in situations where there is interest in the business plan but a lack of experience on the management team.

Social Responsibility

Having a positive company image and a reputation for being socially responsible can often build trust with both customers and potential employees. Every business should plan to attempt to perform at least a minimal amount of community service. Activities could include food drives and working with Habitat for Humanity.

Community activities are known to be some of the best morale and rapport builders. Many people would be surprised to learn how much closer you can become to someone after feeding the homeless together.

Financials

It is common practice for potential investors to review the financials immediately after reading the executive summary. Many investors will only consider companies that have the potential to return large profits or support a successful initial public offering. A strong financial section that projects realistic and sustainable growth will likely encourage potential investors to consider the business plan as a whole.

The financial section should mention your accounting structure and should include income statements, an assumption sheet, balance sheets, cash-flow projections, and a breakeven analysis for at least three years. The income statements and cash flow statements should have monthly projections for the first year and quarterly projections for years two and three. The balance sheet should have quarterly projections for the first year and annual projections for years two and three. If the business has a history, annual financial statements for the previous three years should be also included.

The assumption sheet should be next to the projected income statements. The purpose of an assumption sheet is to provide readers with the basis for the plan's financial projections. The assumption sheet explains how you arrived at most of your numbers and should have several components, including expectations for economic growth, industry growth, sales volume, and market share.

The breakeven analysis shows how much revenue must be generated in order to cover all of the business related expenses, which include both fixed and variable costs. Fixed expenses generally stay the same every month and include rent, utilities, business insurance, and employee salaries. Variable expenses can include sales commissions, cost of inventory, shipping, and other expenses that are related to the product or service and fluctuate on a regular basis.

To determine how much revenue is required to break even, determine your fixed expenses and divide it by the difference between the average unit selling price and its variable costs. For example, let's assume that your business has only $20 in monthly fixed expenses, the average product sells for $10 each, and the average variable costs related to each item total $6. After subtracting the $6 in variable expenses from the $10 unit price, divide the $20 from fixed expenses by the $4 that is remaining after subtracting variable costs from the unit selling price. In this scenario, the breakeven point wouldn't be reached until five units are sold at an average of $10 each. The breakeven formula for this business would resemble the following: $20/($10-$6) = 5.

One of the most important parts of the financial section is the source & use of funds. Most investors want to be convinced that any investments that are made into the company are going to be used to grow the business and not for paying the entrepreneur a salary or to service any pre-existing debt of the company.

The source & use of funds should also detail all sources of investment to date and the total amount of funding that the business is seeking from investors. Investors generally appreciate it when an entrepreneur commits a substantial amount of his own money or when a reputable investor has already taken a financial stake in the company. Investors, however, generally lose interest if it is discovered that the entrepreneur is not fully aware of his actual financial needs. An entrepreneur not requesting enough capital can often times be just as detrimental as an entrepreneur stating that he plans to use the majority of investor funds to pay himself a salary.

Milestones

Every business plan, especially those used to solicit funding, should include a milestone section that has at least four or five concrete objectives that the company can use to measure its progress. A milestone list could include adding locations, introducing new products, or revenue targets. For businesses that have a history, milestones already achieved should be included.

Exit Plan

Every investor wants to know how he will receive his desired return on investment. The exit plan describes the end game. Possible exit options include going public, being acquired by a larger company, merging with another entity, or allowing the business to be an asset for heirs. It is a good idea to seek investments from investors that are likely to be accepting of your exit plan. For example, some investors take equity when they believe the company will be acquired by a larger company. Others, on the other hand, will only invest in companies that have a realistic chance of having a successful initial public offering.

The Appendix

Although a business plan should provide all of the essential information to understanding the business, the appendix is a good place to include complimentary information, such as copies of endorsements, key contracts, letters of intent, and photos of new products. If the appendix is longer than the business plan, I recommend binding the two separately. A long appendix combined with a short business plan may discourage investors from reading the plan if it appears that the majority of the binder is the actual business plan.

Last Words

Preparing a solid business plan is essential for any business that plans to grow and become successful. It is a good idea to hire an accountant to help with choosing an accounting method and organizing the various financial forms. If an entrepreneur is unable to hire a private accountant, I recommend utilizing the assistance of former executives from SCORE that have substantial financial experience.

In addition to helping an entrepreneur determine how to best operate his business, going through the planning process will often make an entrepreneur aware that starting a particular business is a bad idea and, if heeded to, will save the entrepreneur a ton of time and money.

Chapter 11

Marketing & the 4 P's

Marketing is the tool that is used to introduce your product or service to the consumer and ultimately build a household brand name for that product or service. Some of the most reputable companies in the world have used solid marketing plans to build their brands and eventually place their businesses in a class above the competition.

For example, Nike, who is the largest athletic shoemaker in the world, got that way from great marketing and promotion. In the mid-eighties, Nike practically made Michael Jordan, who became the greatest player to ever play the game of basketball, the face of Nike. At the time, Michael Jordan gave Nike a reputation for helping athletes fly or stay in the air a little longer than everyone else. With that, Nike made a fortune with its Nike Air brand even if the shoe wasn't directly related to Michael Jordan.

Even if a person couldn't afford to purchase the Michael Jordan Nike shoe, he still wanted to be associated with Nike in any way that he could and, shortly thereafter, Nike became the athletic shoe of choice for both young and older consumers. Recently over the last few decades, Nike has done a great job of grabbing other talent, such as LeBron James and offering him a mega $90 million endorsement deal.

Many outsiders didn't understand why Nike paid him so much money, and that is because they didn't understand marketing and the importance of a business branding its product. Nike understands that even if the LeBron James shoe doesn't make the company $90 million in profit over the term of the deal, the company will make its profit from the branding that he will continue to provide for the shoe maker in associating Nike with world-class athletes.

This concept will surely make Nike much more than $90 million over time and will be the main reason why Nike maintains its position as the number one athletic shoe maker. Many other shoe companies don't believe in paying top dollar for world-class athletes, as they only consider what that athlete will provide as far as his particular shoe sales instead of the bigger picture, which is the branding effect that the athlete's affiliation will have for the shoe company.

It is important to note that marketing is more than just advertising, the same way that a house is more than just a kitchen. Advertising is indeed a part of marketing, but the concept of marketing expands far beyond just advertising.

Target Market

When marketing, the main goal is generally to reach a specific market. A market can be described as a collection of existing or potential customers who have the desire and ability to buy a specific product or service. The specific market that is sought after by a particular business or marketing plan is considered the target market.

Most businesses start with a single target market that expands strategically in order to gain a larger market share. A good marketing plan will state one target market as well as the effect that market will have on other markets once reached. Having a clearly defined target market is very important before starting any business, and it doesn't matter if it is a product or a service that you need to sell in order to make a profit.

A target market should include a group of people that have the desire and ability to buy a product or service. For example, if starting a restaurant that specializes in low-fat hamburgers, the target market could be health-conscious consumers between the ages of 25 and 40 on the north side of Austin, TX.

If starting a book publishing company that writes mostly business books, the target market could be business students across the country between the ages of 18 and 25. Once a target market is defined, the marketing plan should detail exactly how the product or service will get introduced to that market and what will be done to persuade that market that the product that's being offered is worth the price that is being charged for that product.

Generally, the target market of a business grows when the original market has been captured and the company is meeting the sales goals that were planned when the target market was defined. Often, a company will break into a new market unintentionally.

For example, let's say the target market of a book publishing company was urban women between the ages of 15 and 24. Because of the known relation between women and men in this age group, males in this age group could become a new market as they become curious of what their significant others are reading. This could very well lead to another market being created as the younger brothers of the older members of the 15 to 24 crowd may become curious of what their big brothers are reading.

When it comes to defining an initial target market, it should be a group that will likely openly receive your product or service as well as a group that will have some sort of influence on another market. That way you can kill at least two birds with one stone and expand into other markets without any direct attempts to do so.

Reaching the Target Market

In addition to having a defined target market, an entrepreneur must have the means to efficiently communicate his message to the group. Facebook advertising services have made it very easy for entrepreneurs with limited advertising budgets to deliver messages to their target markets. Facebook advertising permits a marketing campaign to target users by age, gender, marital status, interests, education, and location.

Google's advertising services also permit a business to effectively reach its target market with limited advertising budgets. Google often offers promotions for its advertising services, which provide free or bonus advertising bucks to its users.

The Four P's

One of the best known marketing concepts in business is the four P's. This is also commonly referred to as the controllable marketing factors as they are the aspects of marketing that can be controlled by a company's marketing department. Not all marketing factors can be controlled by a company as a lot of marketing is done by word of mouth.

In business school, one of the first things learned in marketing class is the concept of the four P's. The four P's are product, price, promotion, and place. Some add a fifth element, which is packaging, but I consider that to be a part of the product.

Product

The product or service that a company has to offer will generally make or break a business. You can have the best advertising in the world, but if the product isn't any good, the product won't be purchased multiple times by the same consumer and generally it will be complained about.

The product or service that is offered is the vital point of any business idea. Before doing any type of business or marketing plan, a good product or service that has a high demand needs to be created. To keep it simple, without a good product there is no business or at least there shouldn't be one.

Price

The price of a product is very critical. Just as having a good product is very important, the price of that product is equally as important, and a poorly priced product can be just as bad as having a poor product itself.

Many times a company will have a great product or service to offer but it will be priced without consideration of the spending ability of the target market. For example, if I were writing a book on the steps to escape poverty, it would be unwise to price the book at $39 since many people in poverty wouldn't be able to afford spending that much money on a book, especially when the need to get food is the more immediate concern.

On the other hand, a great product can be underpriced and cause a business to fail. When deciding the price of a product, one must consider all costs associated with producing and promoting that product as well as the contribution that the sales of that product will have toward the overhead of the business.

When evaluating the price of a product, if it appears that the product needs to be priced at a cost that is higher than what the competition is currently selling the same product for, it generally is a strong sign that the business idea needs to be reevaluated. When this happens, it means that the consumer need that you are attempting to supply is already being met at a price that you can't afford to compete with.

Promotion

The proper promotion of a product is equally as important as proper pricing and having a good product. A business can have the best product at the lowest price in the world, but if no one knows about what the business has to offer, the business will likely fail due to a lack of customers.

For example, I can have a car dealership that sells Cadillac Escalade trucks for $500. That's right, $500. This is obviously a great product at a ridiculously low price. However, if no one knows about it, it is likely that I won't sell any vehicles unless someone stumbles upon my car dealership by accident.

Place

Similar to how having a good product with a proper price and having good promotion is critical to the success of a business, it is very important to have the product available in the right place. The internet has made it much easier to make products accessible to target markets. I think it is a good idea to have most products available for purchase online. One of my favorite scenarios is when someone spreads the word about a product to someone in a different geographic location and the product becomes in demand by consumers in the new market. In this scenario, having the product available online will make it possible to service this new market that may be 500 miles away.

A business can have the perfect product, but if the product is not in a place where it can be easily accessed by the target market, failure may be right around the corner. For example, if I were selling high-end business suits targeted toward wealthy consumers, it would be unwise to only have this product for sale in impoverished communities as it would create a barrier for my target market to access my product. Having a product in the right place is very important and can make or break a business idea or company as a whole.

Consumer Decision Making Process

When putting together a good marketing plan, it is very important to understand the psychology of a consumer as he decides to purchase a particular product or service. The first step in the consumer purchasing process is that he recognizes that he has a need for a particular item or service. This can occur from waking up to the feeling of thirst, having a cough, finding an empty cereal box in the food closet, and many other things can trigger this recognition of a need.

After a particular need is recognized, consumers usually perform an internal search as they try to remember how they last fulfilled the same need when it emerged. If no good experiences can be remembered, the consumer will move on to do an external search and ask friends and family for information as well as seek other sources that provide information on the product or service that is being craved.

After the consumer has done his proper research, either mentally or physically on the computer, he will compare all of his reasonable options and look for the best value and all around choice. I was once told in psychology class as an undergraduate student that a person decides to have a relationship with someone or something by evaluating the benefits, the cost, and the availability of competing relationships. This is very similar to what a consumer does at this stage in the process.

After evaluating the options available, the consumer will eventually come to a decision and make a purchase. At this point, he will then decide whom to buy it from, which is very important as a business needs to be ready to position itself to be the place where the product or service is purchased from.

After the purchase and consumption of a product, the consumer will generally create an opinion of the experience and store it mentally for later use when the same need reappears in the future.

Word of Mouth

Word of mouth marketing is probably the best marketing there is for a business that offers a good product or service; however, it can be a nightmare for a business with a bad product. Word of mouth has been the bread and butter for many companies. Believe it or not, word of mouth is practically inevitable since after a product is consumed, the opinion that is created is usually shared with anyone who will listen.

This is the case if the opinion formed is positive or negative. Generally, when the experience is negative, the consumer will tell many more people than he would if the experience had been a good one. It is sometimes true when they say that people feed off of negative energy.

80/20 Rule

The 80/20 Rule states that 80% of all sales and profits will come from 20% of the items or customers. This is very important to know as it helps you focus your business efforts on particular customers and products. Customers that do 80% of the spending deserve much more attention from marketers and managers.

Likewise, an item that provides 80% of the sales should be given more attention and should be strongly monitored to make sure that it is always in stock. Although all customers are important and should be treated with respect, it is not wise to spend a lot of time on customers who don't have the ability to do a large amount of purchasing.

Last Words

How a company plans to reach its target market is a very important topic that must be covered before a company opens its doors for business. If you define a target market and carefully consider the four P's, marketing can be the bread and butter of any business that has wishes to grow and become profitable.

Chapter 12

Human Resources

In my opinion, people are the best resource and most valuable asset when looking to build an empire. In order to utilize and make the most out of this resource, it is critical that you understand human beings for who they are, what they do, and what they believe.

We've all had our experiences with different types of people. As employees, we often have little to no choice regarding the people that we have to work with. However, as an entrepreneur, the power is yours to work with only those who you are comfortable working with. I've often heard people say that they don't like to work with people. However, it is my belief that they just don't like the people that they've worked with. It's a difference and a very valuable one at that.

One of the benefits of being an entrepreneur is that you are the boss. With the exception of some government regulations and requirements, you can pretty much do business as you choose and can also choose with whom it is that you do business with.

I must note that I am not okay with any form of illegal discrimination, whether it is based on race, religion, gender, color, creed, age, disability, or anything else that the government has prohibited. However, the one form of discrimination that I can concur with is that based on character.

As an entrepreneur, it is essential to choose only the best people to work with as the wrong people will be your downfall every time. I would prefer someone with a bachelor's degree and good character over someone with an MBA and bad character. The reason being is the power of synergy. Synergy is when $1 + 1 = 3$ or 4. The two individual parts, when together, are greater than what they could have been individually.

For example, if Fred and Sam could each make $50,000 in sales when working alone and together as a group they only make $100,000, this is not synergy. It is instead wasted energy. However, if when teamed up they could create $150,000 or $200,000 in sales, this is synergy as the sum of the two parts when working together is greater than the sum of the two parts when working individually.

People often only speak of synergy in positive terms, but it is even more powerful when working as a negative force. For example, if two employees of bad character could each discourage 10% of your workforce, it is highly probable that together they could possibly discourage 50 to 100 percent of your workforce. So in this case, 10% + 10% would equal 50% or greater.

This is why only having people of the highest character on your team is essential. The best people will team up and ensure that your company is a success, while those of low character will team up and ensure that your company comes tumbling down. In order to understand people, you must first understand what drives them.

Maslow's Hierarchy of Needs

Abraham Harold Maslow was an American psychologist, who is mostly known for diagnosing the forces that drive human behavior. His theory, which is found in most psychology and some business textbooks, is titled "Maslow's Hierarchy of Needs."

The needs are listed in order of importance and his belief is that the more important needs are the priority to the person until fulfilled. Once fulfilled, the person shifts his priority up the hierarchy. From most to least important, the needs are physiological needs, safety and security, love and belonging, esteem needs, and self-actualization.

Physiological Needs

The most important on the list is a person's physiological needs. These needs would include food, water, shelter, and the ability to breathe. These needs must be met before a person thinks of where to go for vacation or finding new friends. Just think, if you were hungry and haven't eaten any food in days, how likely is it that you're going to worry about who likes you or even if you like yourself at that point? Your only mission is going to be to find food and to attain it by any means necessary.

Safety and Security Needs

After a person's physiological needs are met, it is human nature to then seek out safety and security. This only becomes a priority after the person's physiological needs are met because when a person is lacking food or the ability to breathe, he doesn't care about safety and he will often engage in unsafe behavior to fulfill his needs.

Safety and security includes safety from physical harm and sometimes may include being secured in one's financial space. It is true that it is difficult for people to reach their full potential when they do not feel safe and secure, especially in their homes and neighborhoods of residence. At this stage, a person's focus is generally on survival.

Social Needs

Once a person has a sense of safety and is secure in the space that he's in, human nature calls for him to focus on his social needs, which are also described as the need to be loved and the need to belong. This would include having successful friendships and family relations. Although this is third on Maslow's list, I know personally of people who successfully bypass this step in order to reach levels four and five. However, since business is a team sport where synergy counts for actual points, those who have taken the time to develop meaningful social networks are often in a better position to succeed.

Esteem Needs

Esteem needs are very important and would include the need to have a healthy self-esteem, confidence, and self-respect. In order to reach this goal, many people will join various organizations, write books, become preachers, basketball players, or anything else that can remind or inform them that they have value and are worth something. It is my opinion that you must first convince yourself that you are worth something before someone else can contribute to your self-esteem.

Self-Actualization

This is a person's need to be the best that he can be. The need for self-actualization is probably what led Kobe Bryant, during his prime, to start his daily workouts before most other players. He believes that with enough hard work, there is no reason why he can't become the best basketball player of all time. Many psychologists believe that in order for people to reach this level they need their aesthetic needs satisfied.

Aesthetic needs would include the need to be in the presence of beautiful things, such as nature or someone you find attractive of the opposite sex. It is my opinion that many business people with large ambitions will often marry beautiful women even when it's questionable if the person loves them or not. This is because the person's beauty is an asset to them and may even provide a busy person with a peace of mind, which is often needed to achieve one's ultimate goals in life. I do not, however, recommend dating someone simply because of physical features.

It is important to be aware of this hierarchy because it may give you the solution to why your top salesman is underperforming or why your secretary appears to be depressed or lonely. For example, if half of your staff is from out of town and without friends, it would be a good idea to organize an employer-sponsored community service event. This will increase the chance of having a happy workforce, which usually leads to happy customers.

When to Hire Employees

It is my strong belief that you should only hire employees when you need them. No matter the field of business you are in, if you can satisfy the demands of the business personally or with the help of your business partners, no staff should be hired.

This is very important to the success of your business because it is very possible that if you can handle the demands of the business on your own that there may not be enough business activity to create enough revenue to support a workforce. However, if you have so much business that you can no longer serve all of your customers on your own, it may be time to hire temporary, part-time, or possibly even full-time help.

Payroll Services

If and when you find yourself in a position where help is needed, I do recommend that you use one of the major payroll services offered through either Paychex or ADP. Both companies will print payroll checks with funds taken from the company's account and will subtract all appropriate taxes from the employee's check.

This is a very valuable service and should be used to keep the entrepreneur from spending time trying to figure out tax formulas when he should be looking for new business. It is important to remember that as a president of your own company, your time is valuable and should be used on tasks that will add significant value to the company.

Morale

In my opinion, the key to having an all-for-one attitude in the workplace is having employees with high morale. When your employees have high morale, they will often strive and go the extra mile to impress management, to make sure customers are satisfied, and to make sure that their work is completed at a high level.

On the other hand, employees with low morale will often talk bad about the job, their co-workers, customers, and management. This will then decrease the morale of the employees around that associate and before you know it, no one is happy anymore. This is often a challenge that is not handled well by many business people.

The best way to overcome these types of obstacles is to nip it in the bud. If you hear an employee speaking badly about management or the company, respectfully pull that employee to the side and find out what is bothering that associate.

The key here is to listen carefully. Also, do not attempt to minimize his feelings by making him feel as though what he is upset or discouraged about is unimportant because obviously it's important to him.

Also, try your best to respectfully minimize negative gossiping. Bad talk and gossiping in the work place are disasters waiting to happen. It's hard to have synergy in the work place if your employees don't like each other and can't wait to do harm to one another. As an entrepreneur or executive, it is important that you play the role of a mediator at times and that you demonstrate leadership by positive example.

Last Words

Be careful when making hiring decisions, and then be even more mindful of how you treat and respond to the needs of the staff. Your people are critical to your business and are your most valuable asset. Could Walmart be the powerhouse that it is today if Sam Walton were still alive and he alone were the corporation's only employee?

Chapter 13

Mergers & Acquisitions

After building a successful business, many entrepreneurs find themselves in a position where growth appears as if it would be more efficiently gained by either acquiring or merging with another company.

On average, more companies become strapped for cash in bad economic times but many have great technologies or client bases that are worth acquiring and because of their financial concerns can be acquired at discounted prices. Perfectly healthy companies can also be purchased at deep discounts during bad economic times due to a lack of other buyers and, therefore, a lack of leverage for someone looking to sell.

When an entrepreneur or executive makes the decision to acquire or merge with another company, he will usually contact the target company's CEO. In some cases, the target company's CEO is disinterested in talks. If this is the case, this would generally be the end of the process with this company. However, if there is mutual interest in doing a deal, the buyer will request an executive summary from the target company.

The executive summary provides basic information about the company, such as its financial history and projections, market share, number of locations, and other general information about the business. A good executive summary will encourage the buyer to learn more about the target business without disclosing any confidential information.

Assuming the executive summary is able to keep the attention of the buyer, the two will usually agree to sign a confidentiality agreement, which is also known as a nondisclosure agreement. This will prevent either party from disclosing information that's discovered during negotiations and due diligence. A good nondisclosure agreement will prevent either party from alarming suppliers or employees that a merger or acquisition is taking place, which may result in downsizing.

After securing signatures on the nondisclosure agreement, the target company will produce what is referred to as an offering document or a deal book. The goal of the offering document is to present enough information to encourage the buyer to submit an indication of interest. The offering document discloses financials, key assets, contracts, suppliers, employees, and other important information.

Assuming the buyer still has interest after reviewing the offering document, the buyer submits a nonbinding indication of interest to the target company. The indication of interest details the source of purchasing funds and indicates a price range that the buyer would be willing to pay for the company.

If the seller finds the price range and other details included in the indication of interest to be acceptable, the management teams from both companies will usually meet to provide financial and operational updates. The main goal of the meeting is to persuade the buyer to submit a nonbinding letter of intent, which includes the actual purchasing price. The letter of intent, however, does leave many of the legal details to be worked out during the negotiation of the purchase agreement. One of the most valuable clauses of a letter of intent, if granted, is an exclusivity clause, which prevents the target company from shopping the company to other potential buyers while the buyer conducts its due diligence.

The due diligence process is both time consuming and expensive and will include substantial investigations into the respective businesses. This will include auditing financial statements and verifying the validity of everything disclosed by the target company's management team. Most of the information that the target company will provide to the buyer will likely be maintained in a secure online data room, which permits all key parties, such as lawyers and accountants, to view the information remotely.

Toward the later stages of due diligence, the parties will negotiate the details of the purchase agreement, which is the binding document. The purchase agreement includes the purchase price, any escrow arrangements, amount of cash at closing, and a host of representations and warranties that mostly protect the interests of the buyer. The most common representations and warranties include a guarantee that the seller is the actual owner of the company being sold, the company is current with its tax obligations, and that there are no legal claims involving the company that are unresolved.

After the details of the purchase agreement have been worked out, the companies present the agreement to their respective board of directors, who almost always determine the fate of any M&A deal. There are several M&A transactions that are worth discussing. In this chapter, we will discuss mergers, asset acquisitions, stock acquisitions, and leveraged buyouts.

Mergers

In a merger transaction, two or more companies merge and become one. Mergers will often occur between firms of similar size as companies usually acquire companies that are much smaller and don't bother to merge with them since it dilutes the voting power of their shareholders. The following is a brief overview of the Delaware merger process. It is important to know that a corporation's bylaws can often dictate many of the requirements for executing

M&A deals. The general formalities described are the default rules when the bylaws are silent on the subject.

Delaware Merger Process

Although processes may vary slightly by state, Delaware is the most popular state for M&A activity and is where most large corporations are incorporated. To perform a merger between two Delaware corporations, the board of directors of both corporations must pass a resolution approving the agreement of merger and must issue a statement declaring its advisability. After board approval, both corporations must submit the agreement of merger to their shareholders for a vote to ratify, which requires a majority of all shareholders who are eligible to vote. A summary of the agreement is filed with the Delaware secretary of state and a certificate of merger is issued to the surviving corporation.

At closing, the surviving corporation issues a pre-determined amount of its shares to the shareholders of the dissolving corporation. The dissolving corporation transfers all of its assets to the surviving corporation, which assumes all debts and liabilities of the dissolving corporation.

Exceptions to Voting Procedures

If the shareholders of the surviving firm would have the same rights, preferences, and privileges post transaction and their shares are not diluted by more than 20%, the shareholders of the surviving firm would not have the right to vote to ratify the merger agreement. This is known as the 20% rule.

Short-form mergers provide for another exception to the voting requirements. A short-form merger takes place between a parent company and a subsidiary when the parent owns more than 90% of the voting stock of the subsidiary. If a subsidiary is being merged into a parent company, neither company's shareholders have the right to vote to ratify the merger. If the parent company is merging into the subsidiary, the shareholders of the parent company must vote to ratify.

There is also a holding company exception. When a company creates a subsidiary to act as a holding company and that subsidiary creates a subsidiary also and the original corporation that created the first subsidiary merges with the subsidiary created by the holding company, shareholders of none of the three entities are entitled to vote.

Triangular Mergers

As an attempt to minimize the level of risk to the corporation, many times a company will create a subsidiary for the sole purpose of merging with a target company, which will result in a wholly-owned subsidiary of the purchasing company. This is good because in a traditional merger, the debts and liabilities of the target firm are assumed by the surviving corporation. By creating a subsidiary to merge with the target firm instead of merging with it itself, the corporation protects its most valuable assets against unforeseen liabilities created by the target.

Companies will either perform a forward triangular merger or a reverse triangular merger. A forward triangular merger occurs when a company creates a subsidiary and merges it with the target company, therefore, turning the merger target into a wholly-owned subsidiary. In this transaction, the created subsidiary would be the surviving company after merging with the merger target. In a reverse triangular merger, the subsidiary created by the purchaser merges into the target company. In a reverse triangular merger, the target company would be the surviving company after merging with the subsidiary of the purchaser.

Asset Acquisitions

In an asset acquisition, the acquiring firm purchases all (or some) of the assets of the selling firm. The selling firm will continue to exist and its shareholders shall maintain their stock unless dissolved. If dissolved, the corporation will pass proceeds down to its shareholders by way of a liquidating distribution. In an asset acquisition, the selling firm retains all of its debts and liabilities.

Generally, no shareholder vote is required of the purchasing firm even if the purchasing firm issues its debt securities in lieu of cash to acquire the assets of the selling firm. The selling firm's shareholders must approve the asset sale, with limited exceptions.

In Delaware, shareholders of the selling firm are not entitled to a vote unless the company sells all or substantially all of the company's assets. States that have adopted the Model Business Corporation Act use a 25% rule, which states that the selling firm's shareholders are not entitled to a vote if, post-transaction, 25% of the assets and pre-tax income remain.

After an asset acquisition has been completed, the selling firm usually demands a shareholder meeting to vote on dissolution. If the majority of shares that are entitled to vote approve the dissolution, the firm must then file a certificate of dissolution with the secretary of state. The firm is then given three years to wind up the business, pay its liabilities, and distribute any remaining capital to its shareholders.

De Facto Merger

As previously stated, in an asset acquisition, the purchasing firm only buys the assets of the selling firm and the selling firm retains its own debts and liabilities. However, if the court rules that a de facto merger has taken place, the acquiring firm would be liable for the debts and liabilities of the selling firm as if the two firms completed a merger instead of an asset acquisition.

A de facto merger occurs when there has been a continuity of the selling firm. This is attained by using the same or similar management, personnel, assets, and physical location of the seller's firm. A de facto merger also usually requires the selling firm to dissolve, leaving only the purchasing firm, which in turn operates the seller's business as if there has been no change in ownership or management. In a de facto merger, the surviving firm assumes all the debts and liabilities of the selling firm, which is usually more than it bargained for.

Stock Acquisitions

In a stock acquisition, the acquiring firm buys the stock of the target company from its shareholders. The acquiring firm becomes the owner of the target company and the debts and liabilities of the target company remain with the target company since the only change is with ownership of the target company's stock.

Tender Offers

In a tender offer, a bidder who usually seeks control makes a public announcement that he is interested in buying the stock of a corporation for a set price if a minimum number of shares are tendered to a deposit agent within a certain period of time. Tender offers are made directly from the bidder to the target company's shareholders. Tender offers do not require board member approval. A bidder may use a newspaper ad or other advertising to notify shareholders that he is interested in buying.

To encourage participation from shareholders, the bidder will usually offer a premium for the shares. For example, if a company's stock is trading for $20 on the New York Stock Exchange, a bidder may offer $23 per share, which would be a $3 premium.

The laws regarding tender offers require that the offer remain open for at least 20 days and shareholders must have withdrawal rights co-extensive with the offering period. If at any point the bidder extends a price increase, it must also be offered to those who have already tendered their shares.

Leveraged Buyout

In a leveraged buyout, a company will acquire a controlling interest in a target company using mostly borrowed funds. The percentage of borrowed money used to acquire the target may be as high as 95% and in many cases is well over 60%. The assets of the target company are used as collateral for the financing. The majority of leveraged buyouts are done by private equity firms that receive most of their financing from institutional investors.

After buying a controlling interest in the target company, the cash flow from the target company is used to pay the interest payments on the debt issued for financing. This can be very lucrative as a relatively small investment combined with borrowed funds can get a firm control of a very profitable company. The purchasers in a leveraged buyout will often seek to increase profits, which may be done by cutting payroll if the firm is unable to increase revenues.

For this and other reasons, many have bad feelings regarding lever-aged buyouts since downsizing is often the result, especially during economic downturns.

If a company is acquired during a downturn in the economy, chances are it will be acquired at a discount. The perfect scenario for doing a leveraged buyout is to acquire a company with substantial assets, a large operating income, and one without substantial long-term debt.

There are benefits to doing M&A deals, including leveraged buyouts, during both good and bad economic times. During a good economy, you are more likely to grow sales and profits to help repay the debt. During a bad economy, however, the purchase price might be a lot better. For example, if a company had yearly EBITDA (earnings before interest, taxes, depreciation, and amortization) averaging $10 million, the target company may be willing to sell for $40 million in a bad economy.

In a good economy, a company with similar profits may reason-ably request as much as $70 million. However, in a good economy, if the business is in a fast growing industry, a good management team will usually plan and execute a growth strategy, which may double profits before the end of the third or fourth year.

Appraisal Rights

In Delaware, appraisal rights are given to dissenting sharehold-ers in merger transactions and permit them to petition state court for a fair value of their shares in cash. To have appraisal rights, the shareholder must not have voted yes on the merger, must have been a shareholder on the date of demand for an appraisal, and must remain a shareholder on the effective date of the merger.

Each company participating in a merger must inform its share-holders of their appraisal rights. This notice is usually provided along with the notice of shareholder meeting for a vote on the merger. The company must notify the shareholders at least 20 days before the date of the shareholder vote. Any shareholder who wishes to dissent on the issue of the merger and request an appraisal must notify the company in writing before the shareholder's vote that it intends to demand an appraisal.

If the non-dissenting shareholders approve the merger, the company must notify the dissenting shareholders that appraisal rights are available, which must be within 10 days of the merger's effective date. A shareholder wishing to have his shares appraised must file a petition with the court of chancery within 120 days after the merger's effective date.

Last Words

A merger or an acquisition can be a great way to expand your business. It is worth mentioning one last time that the best investments are often available during downturns in the economy, so be prepared for the next downturn by having good credit and as much cash as possible.

Chapter 14

Deal or No Deal: The Basics of Contract Law

A contract is a promise or a set of promises for the breach of which the law gives a remedy. Generally, the remedy for a breach of contract is to put the injured party in as good a position as he would have been in had the contract terms been fulfilled.

Being able to determine if a contract has been formed is very important, and the basics of contract law should be understood by all entrepreneurs, executives, and investors. In addition to entrepreneurs, executives, and investors, contracts are entered into by everyday people on a regular basis. In order for there to be a valid contract, there must be a meeting of the minds and consideration from both parties.

Meeting of the Minds

There must be a meeting of the minds in order for there to be a valid contract. A meeting of the minds, which is also described as having mutual assent, requires the parties to a contract to have the same understanding of the terms of the agreement. A meeting of the minds is usually accomplished when one person makes an offer that is then accepted by the offeree.

Offer

An offer is a manifestation of willingness to enter into a bargain that is made in such a way that a reasonable person would believe that his acceptance will conclude the bargain. It is important to know that vague or ambiguous material terms will prevent an offer from being valid. For example, it would not constitute an offer to tell someone that you will pay him a fair price for his car. However, assuming that the remaining details are reasonably certain, offering $100 for a specific car qualifies as an offer.

An offeree's power to accept an offer can be terminated by a rejection of the offer by the offeree, a counter-offer from the offeree, revocation by the offeror, a lapse of time, or the death or incapacity of either party. Also, an offeree's power to accept an offer is terminated if he is made aware of any definite action taken by the offeror that is inconsistent with the offeror's intention to enter into the proposed contract with the offeree, such as the offeror agreeing to an exclusive deal with a company other than the original offeree.

Acceptance

An acceptance of an offer occurs when there is a manifestation of assent, by the offeree, to the terms offered by the offeror in a manner accepted or required by the offeror. Some offers that are made require performance from the offeree, not a promise, in order to accept. For example, a contract may state that a specific payment is required in order to accept the offer. In this type of scenario, sending a signed contract back without sufficient funds would not constitute a valid acceptance.

It is also important to know that adding or changing the terms of an offer and sending it back signed to the offeror is not an acceptance. It would be considered a counter-offer, which generally terminates the offeree's power to accept the original offer.

Consideration

Consideration is something bargained for, such as a promise, performance, or forbearance, and received by a promisee from a promisor. For example, an agreement to buy a car for $100 has valid consideration from both parties. The car is the consideration from the seller and the promise to pay $100 is the consideration from the other party.

When determining if there has been valid consideration to form a contract, there is no evaluation of the adequacy of the consideration offered, which means that there is no requirement that the consideration offered be equal among the parties. However, past consideration does not constitute consideration, so a past event or performance cannot be the only thing bargained for by one of the negotiating parties. As stated previously, consideration is required from both parties in order to have a valid contract unless there is a valid consideration substitute.

In certain situations, a promise can be enforced without consideration. One of the most popular consideration substitutes is a written promise to pay a debt that is barred by a technical defense, such as the statute of limitations. For example, writing a creditor acknowledging a debt and promising to pay is enforceable against the debtor even though the statute of limitations may have expired.

Promissory Estoppel

Promissory estoppel is a legal doctrine that permits a promise that is made without consideration to be enforced against the promisor if it prevents injustice. In order for such a promise to be enforced against the promisor, the promisor should have reasonably expected the promise to be relied on by the promisee and the promisee must actually rely on the promise to his detriment. The remedy in a promissory estoppel case is whatever justice requires.

The Statute of Frauds

The statute of frauds is an English statute that has been adopted in the United States that requires certain contracts be in writing and signed by the party to be charged in order to be judicially enforceable. Generally, contracts for the sale or transfer of an interest in land, contracts that cannot be performed within one year of their creation, contracts for the sale of goods of $500 or more, contracts made in consideration of marriage, and contracts to answer for the debts of others are covered by the statute of frauds. Also, a contract of an executor or administrator to answer, with his own money, for the duty of the decedent must be in writing to be enforceable against the executor or administrator.

Excuses for Non-Performance

Perfect Tender

When the contract is for the sale of goods, the buyer has the right to reject the goods and withhold payment if the goods or the tender of the delivery fail to conform in any respect to the contract. In such a situation, the buyer also has the right to accept only a portion of the goods and to reject the rest. If a buyer rejects goods from a seller, the seller, assuming time for performance has yet to expire, has the right to notify the buyer of his intention to cure and to then make a conforming delivery. If time to perform has expired, the seller will generally only be able to cure if he had reasonable grounds to believe that the improper tender, possibly with the addition of a money allowance, would be acceptable to the buyer.

Substantial Performance

When a contract is for a service, only substantial performance is generally required from the parties in order to be released from their duties of the contract. Therefore, if one party only substantially performs, the other party is still required to perform. If a contract is for both goods and services, the most dominant element determines if a perfect tender or only substantial performance is required.

Anticipatory Repudiation

When a party to a contract, prior to the required time of his performance, makes a statement or commits an action that makes it clear that he does not intend to perform, the other party may also withhold performance and immediately take legal action for damages. Any repudiating party does, however, have the right to retract his repudiation so long as the other party hasn't materially changed his position since the repudiation or taken other action that indicates that he considers the repudiation final. If a repudiating party does retract his repudiation, he must provide any reasonable assurance demanded by the other party.

Failure to Give Assurance

If reasonable grounds arise to believe that an obligor will commit a breach by non-performance, the obligee may demand adequate assurance that the obligor will perform and, if reasonable, suspend any performance for which he has not already received the agreed exchange until he receives such assurance. If the obligor fails to provide such assurance to the obligee, the obligee may treat the obligor's lack of assurance as a repudiation and seek damages for breach.

Voiding a Contract or Contract Clause

In addition to claiming that an act of fraud has taken place, which was briefly discussed in the business entity chapter, there are many strategies that lawyers utilize to void both clauses and entire contracts. It shouldn't be too hard to believe that some people negotiate in bad faith, which often leads to misunderstandings and unfair surprises. The following are a few defenses to a breach of contract claim.

Mistake of Fact

Generally, when both parties to a contract make a mistake as to a basic assumption of the agreement that has a material effect, the contract is often voidable by the adversely affected party unless he assumes the risk of mistake by agreement or, at the time of the agreement, he is aware that he only has limited knowledge with respect to the facts to which the mistake relates.

It is much tougher to void a contract when only one party has made a mistake. However, in situations where the other party knows or should have known about the mistake, courts are less reluctant to void a contract.

Lack of Capacity

A contract is voidable if a party to the contract lacks capacity, which can be due to being underage, suffering from mental illness or defect, and intoxication. If a person lacks capacity because he is intoxicated, the other party must have reason to know that the intoxicated party is unable to act in a reasonable manner or understand in a reasonable manner the nature and consequences of the transaction in order for the contract to be voidable.

Unconscionability

When a contract, at the time of the agreement, contains clauses that create an unfair surprise and oppressive terms, a court may refuse to enforce the contract or the unconscionable terms. Also, a court may decide to limit the application of any unconscionable term so that it doesn't cause an unconscionable result.

Duress

If a contract has been formed because of an improper threat, such as a threat of violence, and the party under duress had no reasonable alternative, a claim of duress will often make such contract voidable. However, in situations where the improper threat is made by one who is not a party to the contract, the contract is not usually voidable by the victim if the other party to the contract doesn't know of the duress and in good faith gives value or relies materially on the transaction.

Assignment of Contractual Rights and Duties

An obligee usually has the ability to assign his contractual rights, such as the right to receive payment, to another party. Generally, a contractual right can be assigned unless the assignment would materially change the duties of the obligor or a contract clause is present that forbids and invalidates assignments.

Obligors also have the right to delegate duties to others, such as a duty to paint a house or some other form of construction work. However, the delegation of a duty becomes much more difficult when the obligee has a substantial interest in having the obligor perform the act promised, such as painting a special piece of art or singing at the Super Bowl. It is important to also know that the obligor generally remains responsible for his obligation even after delegation.

10 Important Contract Clauses

Depending on the transaction, contracts can be exceptionally long and will usually include a lot of language to protect the interests of one or both parties. Although not all contract clauses are always enforceable, below are some common contract clauses that are present in most contracts.

1. Choice of Law and Forum

Most contracts that are prepared by attorneys include a clause that dictates the state and county of any civil matters that arise from the contract. In addition to describing the location of any future litigation, the language of the contract will also determine which state's laws will be the controlling law for settling any disputes.

2. Statute of Limitations

The statute of limitations determines the amount of time which may pass before the judicial system may no longer be utilized to seek a remedy for a legal claim. Many contracts include clauses that shorten the statute of limitations and are often enforceable if the period is reasonable.

3. Indemnification

An indemnification clause is a provision in which one party agrees to make good for any loss, damage, or liability incurred by another. For example, a buyer of a business will often require an indemnity clause that requires the seller to make good for any liabilities that arise from actions or events that occurred prior to the sale of the business. If you are the party that is promising to indemnify the other party, be sure to negotiate a limit as to the maximum amount that you may be liable.

4. Time of Performance

In contracts where time is of the essence, it is important to include a clause that requires that performance be tendered at a specific time. In a contract with a specific period for performance, a party has breached, and may be sued for breach of contract, if he has not performed his duties at the required time.

5. Arbitration

Arbitration clauses require that any disputes arising from a contract be resolved through binding arbitration, which means that the parties may not use the judicial system as a means to become whole. Negotiating away your right to utilize the judicial system to obtain a remedy should not be done hastily.

6. Liquidated Damages

A contract may stipulate the amount of damages to be recovered in the event of a breach. It is important to know that liquidated damages clauses are generally only valid when, at the time of the contract, the amount of possible damages for any future breach would be difficult to determine and, at the time of contract, the amount of liquidated damages stipulated in the clause is a reasonable forecast of potential damages. Therefore, any liquidation clause that is unreasonable or appears to be a penalty will likely not be enforced.

7. Attorney Fees

A good contract will require the losing party in a breach of contract claim to reimburse the prevailing party for reasonable attorney fees. A clause to pay attorney fees generally deters parties from acting or litigating in bad faith.

8. Merger & Integration

Most contracts will state that the contract document contains the entire agreement and that the parties are not relying on any statements or promises from the other party that are not also included within the document. It is important to make sure that all promises, representations, and warranties are included within the text of the contract, especially when dealing with a contract that has a merger clause.

9. Severability

The severability clause is also referred to as the savings clause, and it protects the enforceable parts of a contract in situations where one or more parts are judicially declared to be void or unenforceable. Savings clauses are extremely important and should be included in every contract.

10. Non-Waiver

A non-waiver clause protects a party who excuses performance from another party and reserves his right to enforce, at a later date, any contract provisions that he may have allowed to go unperformed. However, without a non-waiver clause, it is possible to lose your right to enforce a contract provision that you did not enforce previously. Non-waiver clauses should also be included in every contract.

Last Words

It is very important to understand the basics of contract law, and I recommend that all entrepreneurs and executives purchase and keep handy a copy of the Restatement (Second) of Contracts. One last point to know and remember is to be careful not to include any ambiguous terms when drafting a contract, as most ambiguous contracts are interpreted against the party that drafted the contract.

About the Author

LaFoy Orlando Thomas III, Esq. is an attorney, entrepreneur, and investor. In addition to his law degree from the University of Arkansas School of Law, he holds two business degrees and has been studying business and finance since the age of 14. LaFoy has previously been licensed as a financial advisor and has been featured on various media outlets, including Business Insider, Consumerism Commentary, and Gurufocus.com. Along with business and finance, his passions include economics, politics, and the study and practice of law.

Referenced & Recommended Readings

Books

Abrams, Rhonda. *Successful Business Plans: Secrets & Strategies, Fifth Edition.* Palo Alto, CA: Planning Shop, 2010

Irwin, Robert. *How to Get Started in Real Estate Investing.* New York, NY: McGraw-Hill, 2002

Kiyosaki, Robert. *Rich Dad Poor Dad: What the Rich Teach Their Kids About Money That the Poor and Middle Class Do Not!* New York, NY: Warner Books, 2000

McCrary, Stuart. *How to Create & Manage a Hedge Fund: A Professional's Guide.* Hoboken, NJ: John Wiley & Sons, Inc., 2002

Oesterle, Dale. *The Law of Mergers and Acquisitions, Third Edition.* St. Paul, MN: West, 2005

Websites

Bloomberg
www.bloomberg.com

CNBC
www.cnbc.com

Department of Commerce
www.commerce.gov

Department of Labor
www.dol.gov

Federal Reserve
www.federalreserve.gov

TD Ameritrade
www.tdameritrade.com

Yahoo! Finance
www.finance.yahoo.com

Made in the USA
Las Vegas, NV
16 January 2021

16036709R00118